Blacksmithing for Beginners
20 Essential Hand Forged Projects

Disclamer: All photos used in this book, including the cover photo were made available under a Attribution-ShareAlike 2.0 Generic (CC BY-SA 2.0) and sourced from Flickr

Copyright 2016 publisher - All rights reserved.

This document is geared towards providing exact and reliable information in regards to the topic and issue covered. The publication is sold with the idea that the publisher is not required to render accounting, officially permitted, or otherwise, qualified services. If advice is necessary, legal or professional, a practiced individual in the profession should be ordered.

- From a Declaration of Principles which was accepted and approved equally by a Committee of the American Bar Association and a Committee of Publishers and Associations.

In no way is it legal to reproduce, duplicate, or transmit any part of this document in either electronic means or in printed format. Recording of this publication is strictly prohibited and any storage of this document is not allowed unless with written permission from the publisher. All rights reserved.

The information provided herein is stated to be truthful and consistent, in that any liability, in terms of inattention or otherwise, by any usage or abuse of any policies, processes, or directions contained within is the solitary and utter responsibility of the recipient reader. Under no circumstances will any legal responsibility or blame be held against the publisher for any reparation, damages, or monetary loss due to the information herein, either directly or indirectly.

Respective authors own all copyrights not held by the publisher.

The information herein is offered for informational purposes solely, and is universal as so. The presentation of the information is without contract or any type of guarantee assurance.

The trademarks that are used are without any consent, and the publication of the trademark is without permission or backing by the trademark owner. All trademarks and brands within this book are for clarifying purposes only and are the owned by the owners themselves, not affiliated with this document.

Table of content

Introduction 7
Chapter 1 - Getting Started with Blacksmithing 8
Chapter 2 - Tools and Equipment 10
Forge 10
Bellow 12
Anvil 14
Sledgehammer 15
Cross Peen hammer 15
Cold chisel 16
Hot chisel 16
Hot set 17
Cold set 18
Tongs 18
Fuller 19
File 19
Water bucket 20
Chapter 3 - Raw Materials 21
Mild Steel (Low-carbon steel) 21
Medium-Carbon steel 22
High-Carbon steel 23
Fuels 25

Chapter 4 - Blacksmithing Techniques 26

Managing fire 26

Bending 28

Straightening 32

Drawing down 35

Pointing a rod 36

Drawing ridges 39

Cutting 40

Upsetting the rod 42

Twisting 44

Punching and drifting 45

Fire-Welding 47

Tampering 50

Chapter 5 - Making Your Own Blacksmithing Tools 52

Project 1: Round Punch 52

Project 2: Hot Chisel 57

Project 3: Cold Chisel 61

Project 4: Hot Set 64

Project 5: Cold Set 79

Project 6: Tongs 79

Project 7: Fullers 93

Project 8: Eye Chisel 95

Project 9: Eye Drift 97

Project 10: Cross Peen Hammer 98

Project 11: Ball Peen Hammer 109

Project 12: Claw Hammer 114

Project 13: Anvil 121

Chapter 6 – Making Your Own Carpentry tools 124

Project 14: Chisel 124

Project 15: Plane Iron 129

Project 16: Brace 132

Project 17: Center Bit 141

Chapter 7 – Making Common Home Tools Using Your Own Created Tools 143

Project 18: Knife 143

Project 19: Axe head 148

Project 20: Hoe 155

Conclusion 159

FREE Bonus Reminder 160

Introduction

Blacksmithing is one of the ancient skills that keep on gaining relevance in modern time. It is the skill that introduced the Iron Age, propelled the industrial age and the metallic ornamental age.

Having survivalist skills such as blacksmithing can greatly help you, especially if you are adventurous person and find yourself in a situation where you cannot access modern means of producing basic tools of work.

Blacksmithing helps you cut down on cost of buying tools and common metallic implements. It helps you effectively utilize your free time towards creative endeavor.

Learn blacksmithing tools so that others may learn – Just as I learned so that I could be of benefit to you.

I hope by reading this book you will be able to become a great blacksmith utilizing your backyard space doing great things as I do.

Thank you. Keep reading!

Chapter 1 – Getting Started with Blacksmithing

Blacksmithing is the art and craft of making metallic products through forging. Blacksmithing gained its prominence during the Iron Age (1500BC – to 700BC) when iron replaced bronze as the primary material for making weapons and major tools.

Blacksmithing is associated with the beginning of industrial revolution as it enabled complex machinery and factories to be established, more so, using steel.

Blacksmithing is a profession that has defied ages. It continues to thrive and prosper in modern times. Its needs are just as much as they were during the pre-industrial period, if not more. While industrialization grabbed much of the blacksmithing work from the hands of man, it cannot replace the ingenious creativity of art and craft of blacksmithing of which every blacksmith is uniquely endowed.

Products made from blacksmithing are highly regarded and can fetch several times higher prices compared to the industrial products. Blacksmithing, apart from being a profession, is also an industrious hobby loved by many.

To get started you need to know the right tools, equipment and raw materials required for your blacksmithing endeavor and how to get them. Also you need to master basic blacksmithing techniques so that you can be able to confidently embark on various blacksmithing projects such as those provided in this book.

1.0 A typical smithy

Chapter 2 – Tools and Equipment

The following are important tools and equipment that you will need for your blacksmithing work;

Forge

This refers to the fire setup. It also includes the bellows and the hearth.

There are different kinds of forge setups ranging from traditional to modern. In this book we show DIY (Do-It-Yourself) forges – those that you can later on make on your own with locally available materials once you gain the skills.

Fig. 2.0 forge burner

Fig. 2.1 a simple home-made forge

2.2 another version of home-made forge

Bellow

This refers to the equipment that is used to blow air into the fire. Blowing is important in increasing oxygen supply to the fire thus making the fire burn at a higher temperature.

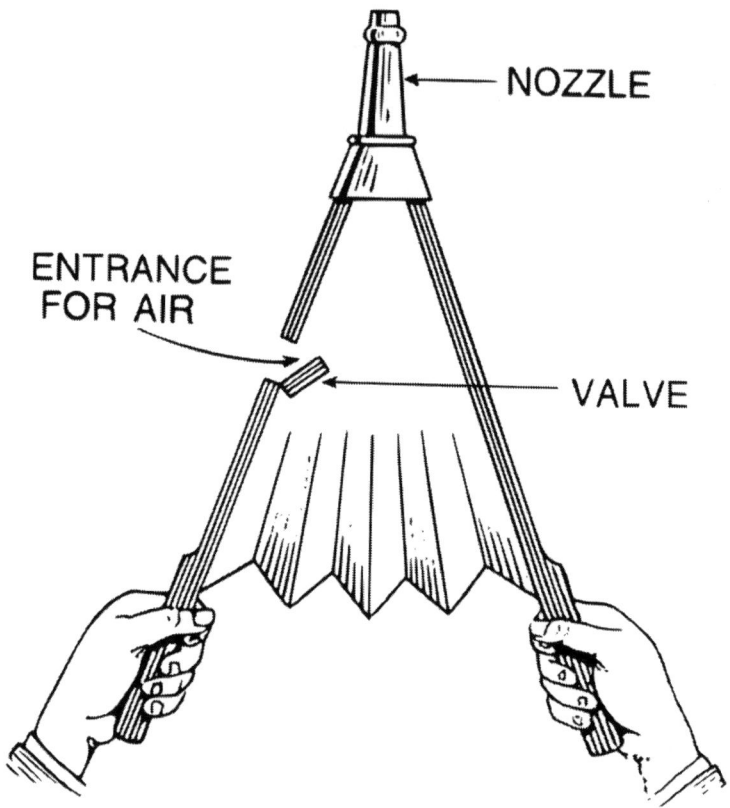

Fig. 2.3 Bellow parts

A traditional bellow appears in Fig. 2.4

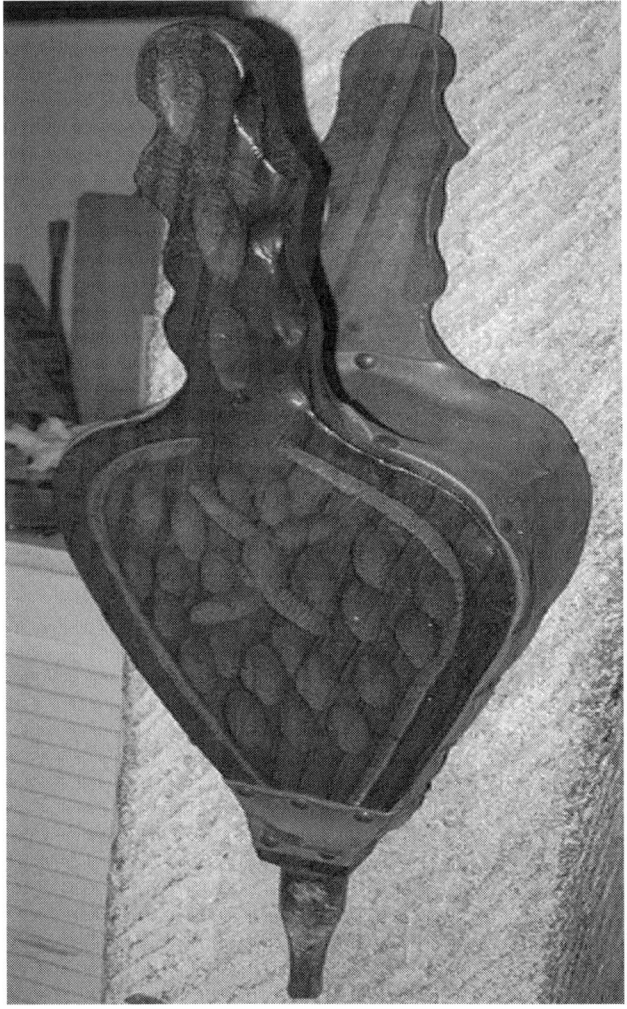

Fig. 2.4 Traditional Bellow

These days, most blacksmiths use improvised commercial blowers such as dust blower for computers or salon blowers for hair.

Fig. 2.1 has a hand-lever blower while fig. 2.2 has a battery-driven dust blower.

Anvil

This is by far one of the most definitive tools for a blacksmith and metalwork in general. It is a platform on which forging is done. It is hard to miss an anvil in a typical metalwork workshop.

Fig. 2.5 shows Anvil and its major parts.

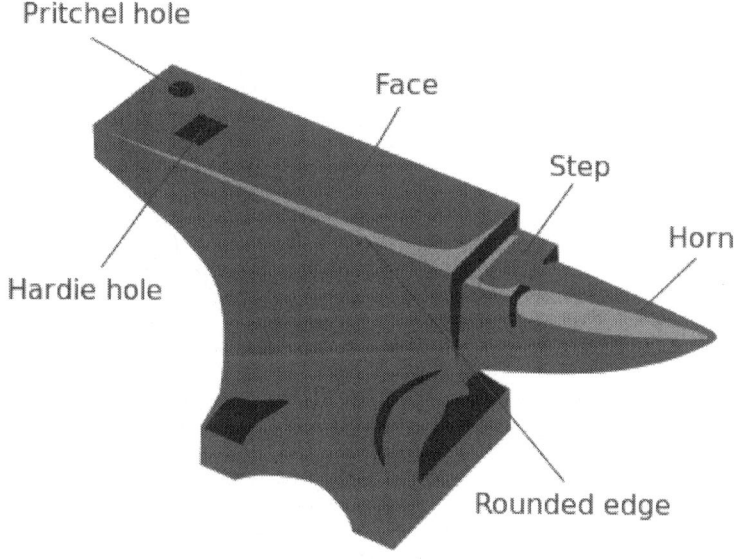

Fig. 2.5 Anvil

Sledgehammer

This is the hammer used for pounding metals during forging.

Fig. 2.6 depicts a typical sledgehammer

Fig. 2.6 Sledgehammer

Cross Peen hammer

This is a hammer that is most widely used to forge metals on anvil.

Fig. 2.7 Cross peen hammer

Cold chisel

This is used to cut cold mild steel. It differs from hot chisel in the sense that its cutting part is hardened and tampered.

Fig. 2.8 Cold Chisel

Hot chisel

This chisel is used to cut hot metal. As such, it is neither hardened nor tampered.

Fig. 2.9 Hot Chisel

Hot set

This is used to cut hot metals

Fig.2.10

Cold set

This is used to cut cold metals

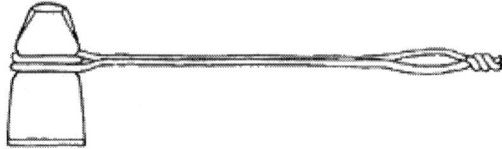

Fig. 2.12

Tongs

These are used to hold metal while it is being forged.

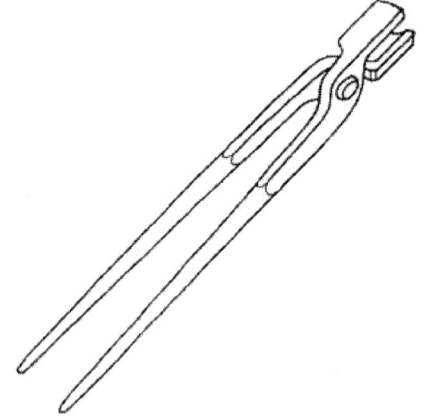

Fig. 2.13

Fuller

This is used to make grooves in hot metals. There are different types of fullers depending on your preference. As such, there is no standard fuller provided that it has rounded edge that makes groove. A typical fuller looks like chisel except that it has round edge.

A simple fuller, like one illustrated in this book is simply made of a round rod bent to form an almost 'Z' shape, but with right angles.

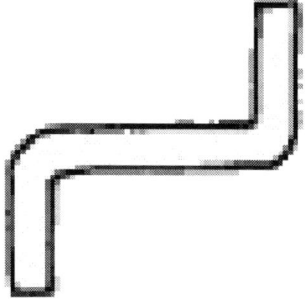

Fig. 2.13

This can then be handled using tongs and driven onto hot metal using a sledge hammer.

File

This is used to sharpen or smoothen out metal during final touches.

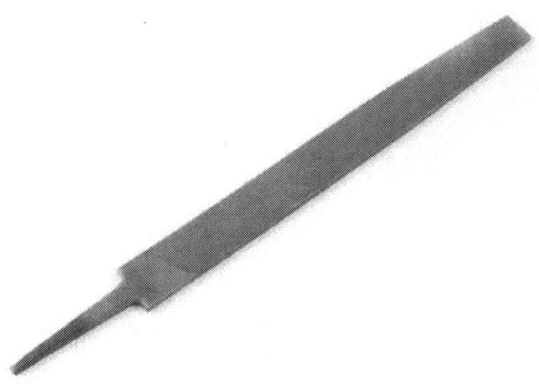

Fig.2.14

Water bucket

This is used for providing water when needed during the forging process.

Fig. 2.15

Chapter 3 – Raw Materials

Most raw materials required for blacksmithing are iron-based, more so, steel. Fuels, water and dyes are also some of the other raw materials that may be required.

Mild Steel (Low-carbon steel)

This is by far the commonest type of steel. It is cheap and easily available. Mild steel contains less than 0.3% carbon. The typical range lies between 0.04% and 0.30%

Some of the common sources of mild steel for your blacksmithing work could be;

- Bar sources of mild steel:
- Reinforcing rods at construction sites (though these have a relatively higher content of carbon)

Sheet sources of mild steel:

- Truck chassis
- Oil drum
- Car body panel

Some of the common uses of mild steel in blacksmithing include;

Bar uses:

- Sickles
- Tongs
- Set handles

Sheet uses:

- Hinges
- Hoes

Unique properties of mild-steel for blacksmithing;

- It is easier to forge and weld
- Can be cut and bend while cold
- Can be forged at bright yellow heat
- Not easy to harden

Medium-Carbon steel

Medium steel contains slightly higher carbon content compared to mild steel. Typical carbon content ranges from 0.31% to 0.60%.

Some of the common sources of medium-carbon steel for your blacksmithing work could be;

- Tractor plough disc
- Vehicle half-shaft
- Plough mould board

Common uses of medium-carbon steel in blacksmithing include;

- Hot chisels
- punches
- hammers
- hoes

Unique properties of medium-carbon steel for blacksmithing;

- Can be forged and welded, though not as easy as mild steel
- Should be forged while a little cooler than mild steel.
- Can be forged at bright yellow heat
- It is easier to harden compared to mild steel

High-Carbon steel

High-carbon steel has one of the highest carbon content. Its carbon content ranges between 0.61% and 1.5%.

Some of the common sources of high-carbon steel for your blacksmithing include;

- Vehicle leaf spring
- Wood saw
- Suspension coil

- Large hacksaw blade
- Anti-roll bar
- Torsion bar

Common uses of high-carbon steel in blacksmithing include;

- Tin snips
- knives
- Axes
- Wood chisels
- Cold sets
- Adze
- Cold chisels
- Plane blades
- Stone and wood carving tools

Unique properties of high-carbon steel for blacksmithing;

- Primarily used for making tools – it is difficult to cut, bend or break
- Can be forged at orange/yellow heat

Fuels

The kind of fuel to use depends on its availability. In rural areas, the most common kind of fuel is charcoal or coal. In urban areas, gas is the most commonly used. Where electricity is cheap, then, it can also be used. So, your choice of fuel largely depends on its availability and affordability.

In this book, we assume charcoal/coal as our own kind of fuel as it is easily available and cheap.

Chapter 4 – Blacksmithing Techniques

Blacksmithing is a skill. Like every other skill, it has its own techniques that make it easy to apply. The following are some of the important techniques/skills that you need to master;

- Managing fire
- Bending
- Straightening
- Drawing down
- Cutting
- Upsetting
- Punching and drifting
- Fire-welding
- Heat treatment?

Managing fire

Fire should be well managed during forging. Different temperature ranges are suitable for different forging materials. Using the right fuel, forge and bellows will ensure that you are able to easily control temperature.

You cannot have exact temperature. However, reading the fire color can enable you to estimate the temperature range. You can then use fire chart to approximate the right temperature range.

Fahrenheit	The Color of the Steel
2000°	Bright Yellow
1900°	Dark Yellow
1800°	Orange Yellow
1700°	Orange
1600°	Orange Red
1500°	Bright Red
1400°	Red
1300°	Medium Red
1200°	Dull Red
1100°	Slight Red
1000°	Very Slightly Red, Mostly Grey
800°	Dark Grey
575°	Blue
540°	Dark Purple
520°	Purple
500°	Brown/Purple
480°	Brown
465°	Dark Straw
445°	Light Straw
390°	Faint Straw

Fig. 4.0 Fire Chart

Different kind of forges can be carried out at different fire ranges;

- Bright yellow (with some whitish sparks) – used for welding
- Bright yellow – used for forging mild steel
- Yellows – used for forging mild steel
- Orange/yellow – used for forging high-carbon steel
- Bright red – used for annealing mild steel
- Medium red – used for annealing or hardening mild steel. Can also be used for bending mild steel.
- Dull red – This is ideal for hardening and annealing high-carbon steel.

Bending

Mild steel can be bent without heating. However, medium-carbon and high-carbon steel will require forging in order to bend.

When bending;

Don't hit the part to be bent directly on the anvil or its edge this will draw it down instead of bending. Extend the part to be bent to the edge of the anvil but hit it just a few millimeters away from the edge. This will allow the metal to bend without drawing down.

To forge prior to bending, heat the part to be bent to a bright-red heat or as indicated in the fire management section for the respective steel type. Make sure that you use bending or leverage blows (hitting at an angle to force bending) rather than mash blows (hitting perpendicular to the iron to force the metal to draw down).

Bending at one edge – round bend;

Step 1: extend iron so that the part to be bent touches the edge of the anvil's horn.

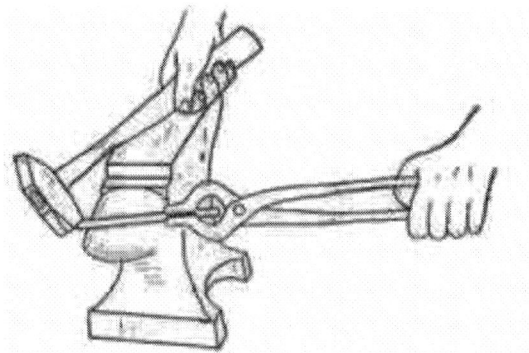

Fig. 4.1

Step 2: continue hammering to bend as you extend the iron rod around the anvil's horn to form circular bend

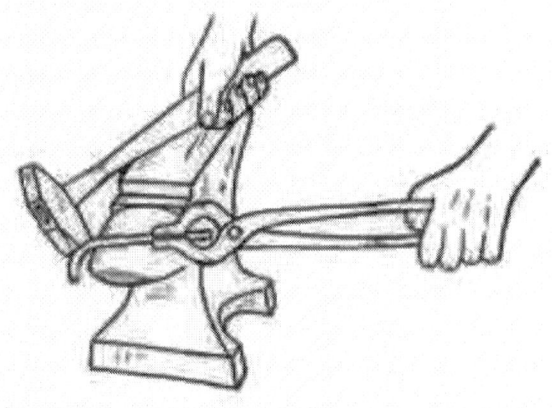

Fig. 4.2

Step 3: Extend the rod further as you continue hammering so as to extend the circular edge.

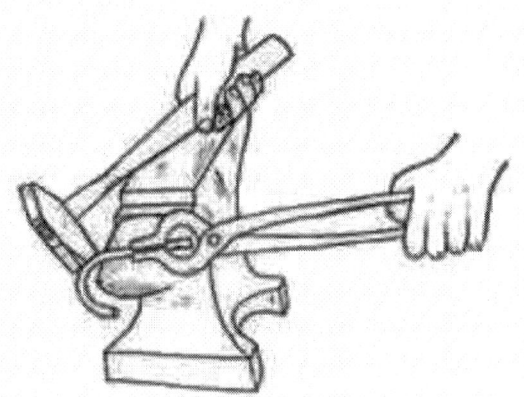

Fig. 4.3

Bending at both edges;

Step 1: use tongs to hold both ends of the rod while the middle of the rod rests on the Anvil's horn

Fig. 4.4

Step 2: apply use your hands to apply even pressure on both ends of the rod as you press them downwards

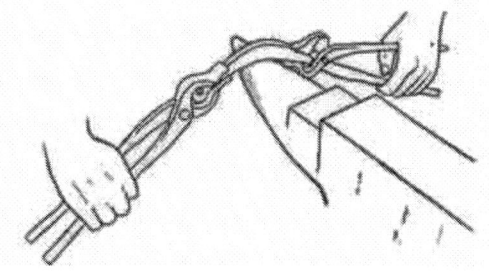

Fig. 4.5

Step 3: put one end of the bent rod into the anvil's hole so that you can bend the rod further using the tongs.

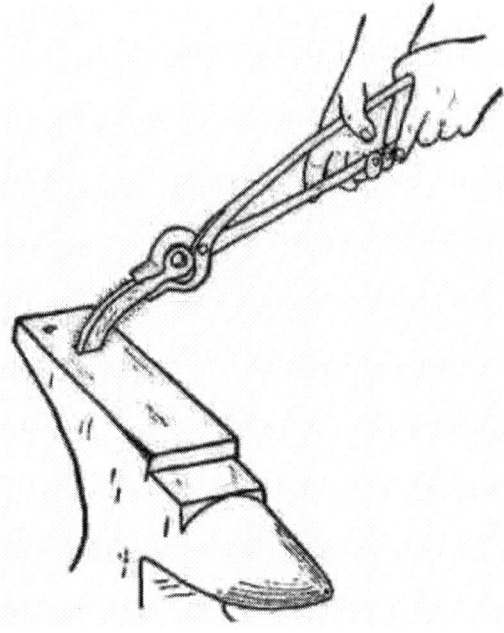

Fig. 4.6

Straightening

Straightening is important, especially when you have to recycle materials such as coil spring and leaf spring required to be used for some projects in this book.

Straightening part of a coil:

Step 1: insert the coil into the anvil horn and pull one edge using tongs towards you while hammering

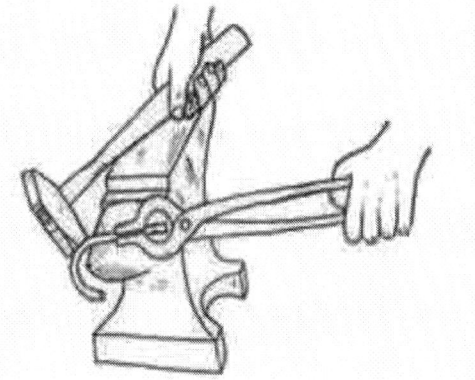

Fig. 4.7 1

Step 2: continue pulling while hammering

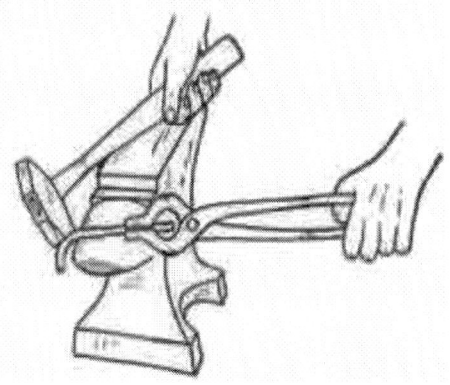

Fig. 4.8

Step 3: put the edge that remains not yet straight and can no longer be straightened by the horse into the anvil hole while push one edge against the bend

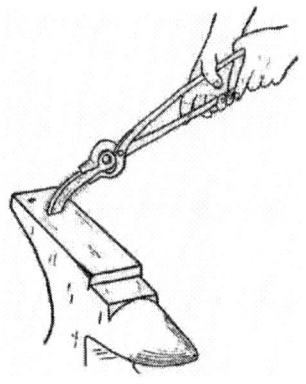

Fig. 4.9

Step 4: lightly hammer the straightened rod from the coil to have an even form.

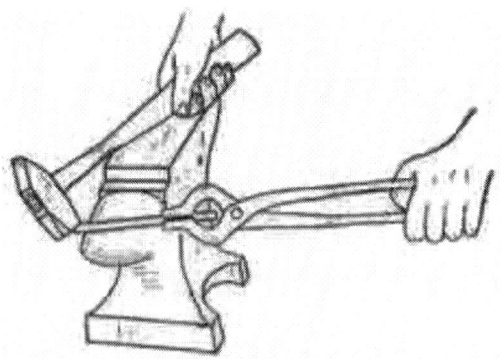

Fig. 4.10

Drawing down

Drawing is the process of elongating and thinning a piece of metal using hammer.

Drawing down the edge;

Step 1 position the edge of the rod that you want to draw down against the edge of the anvil and hammer

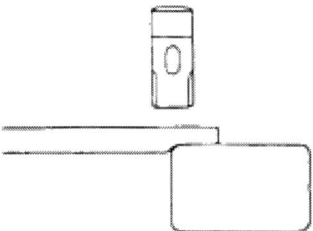

Fig. 4.11

Step 2: change the drawn down side to look up so that you can draw down the opposite side

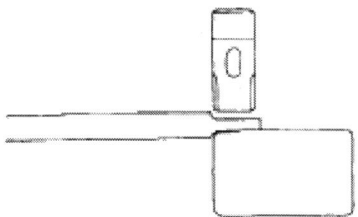

Fig. 4.12

Step 3: To have a narrower draw down in the middle, hammer more towards inner end of the two edges evenly.

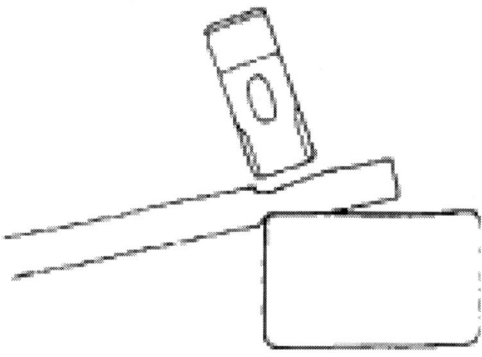

Fig. 4.13

Pointing a rod

Pointing a rod is simply to make it sharper at one end such as for punch or chisel

Flat point (flat chisel);

Step 1: draw down two edges of the rod such that there two flat opposite sides that narrow towards the end like a wedge

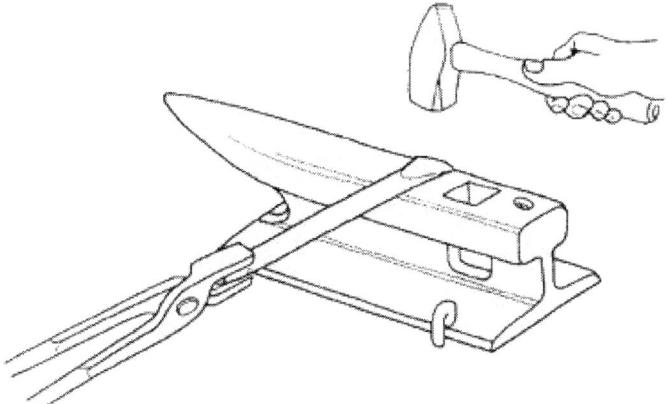

Fig. 4.14

Step 2: hammer the sides of the two edges so as to make them flat

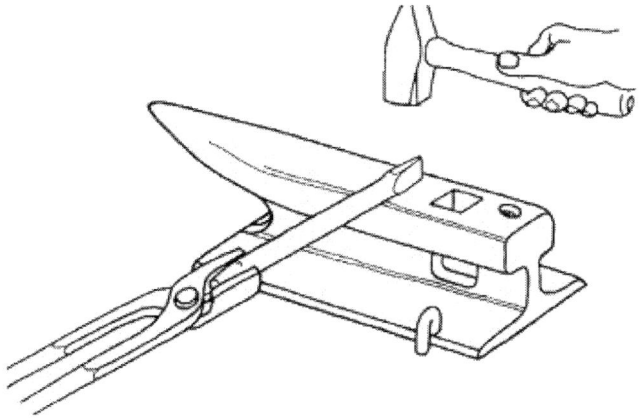

Fig. 4.15

Square point;

In the square point alls edges are equal as opposed to the flat point. Do the same thing as you did for the flat point except that the hammering should be even on all the four edges

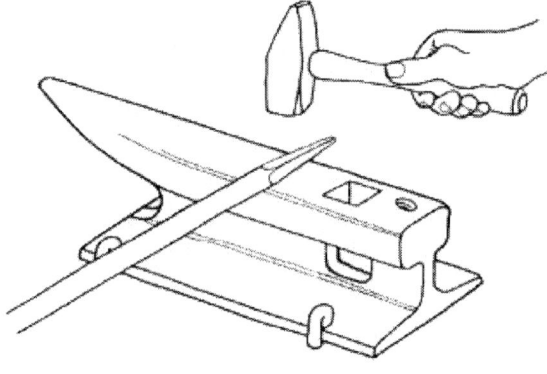

Fig. 4.16

Round point;

First, make a square point. Then, start striking the angles light so that they disappear to form a roundish point. Continue hammering lightly as you roll the rod for an even round.

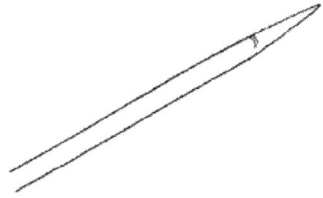

Fig. 4.17

Drawing ridges

Sometimes you may need to draw ridges in a piece of rod or sheet.

You can either opt to use the edge of an anvil or peen hammer, whichever is available and convenient for you.

Using the rounded end of anvil;

Position the rod slanting diagonally against the rounded edge of the anvil. Draw down lightly to form a ridge. Continue with this until you get the required depth and number of ridges.

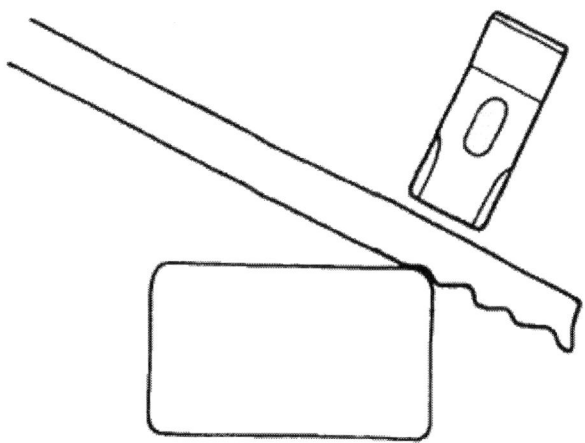

Fig. 4.18

Using peen hammer;

Lay the rod on the anvil. Draw down using the peen side of the hammer to get a ridge. Continue with this until you get the required depth and number of ridges.

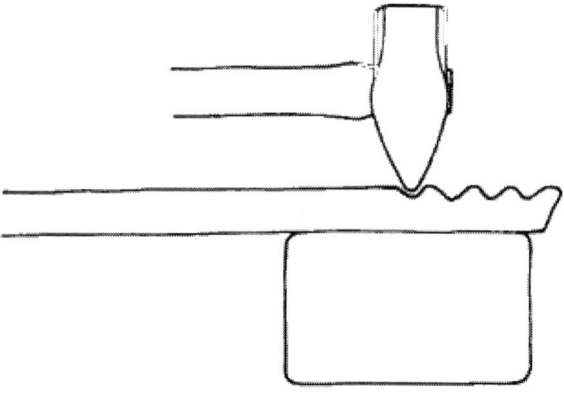

Fig. 4.19

Cutting

You will inevitably need to cut iron into required pieces for your various projects. You can either opt to use a hardy or use cold and hot sets.

Using hardy

Place the hardy on the anvil. Horizontally position the part of the metal that you want to cut onto the hardy. Hammer perpendicularly onto the metal against the hardy

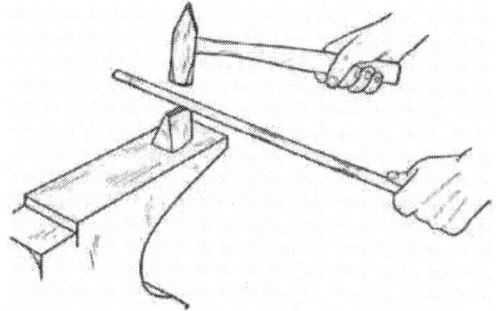

Fig. 4.20

Using cold and hot sets. You can use cold set for cold metals or hot set for forged metal.

Step 1: Mark a line at the point where you want to cut the metal. Position the hot or cold set onto the marked line. Strike the set until the metal forms a deep right almost but not touching the anvil.

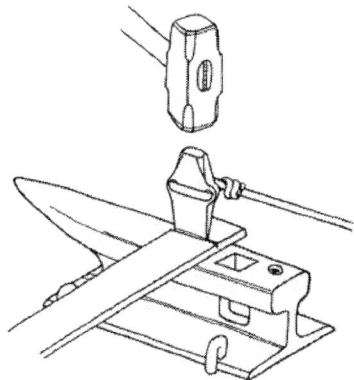

Fig. 4.21

Step 2: Remove the set and hit lightly at the edge of the cutout piece while holding the rest of the metal.

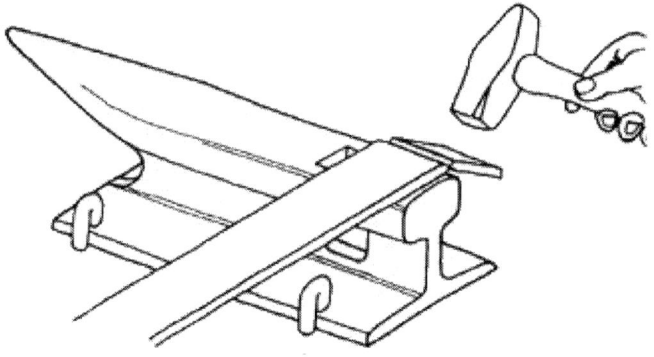

Fig. 4.22

Upsetting the rod

Upsetting refers to increasing the thickness of a metal.

Step 1: forge one end of the rod or the part which you want to upset. Hold the rod to rest vertically perpendicular to the anvil with the forged part resting on the anvil. Hit it lightly as you gradually increase the intensity until the expected point starts bulging. Continue hitting with a hammer until you get the right size of bulge.

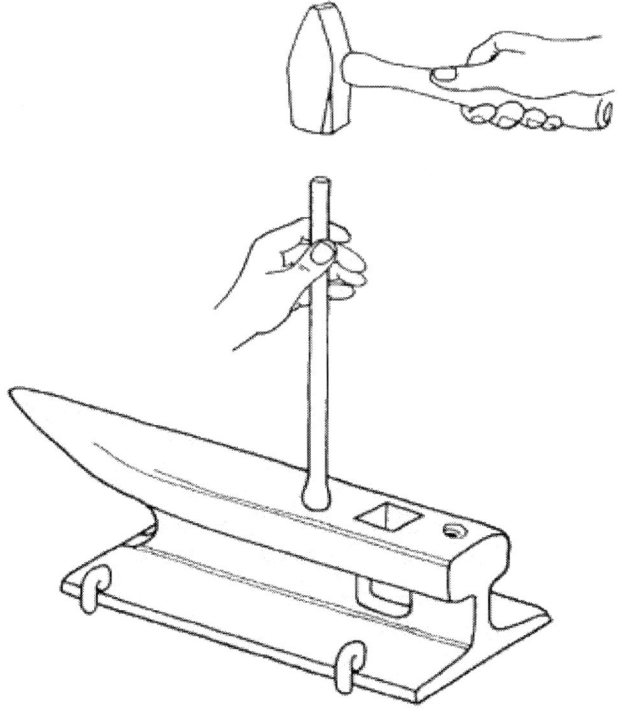

Fig. 4.23

In case you want to upset not the end but a certain point on the rod, forge that point only and make sure that it is closest to the anvil as you position the rod vertically for hitting.

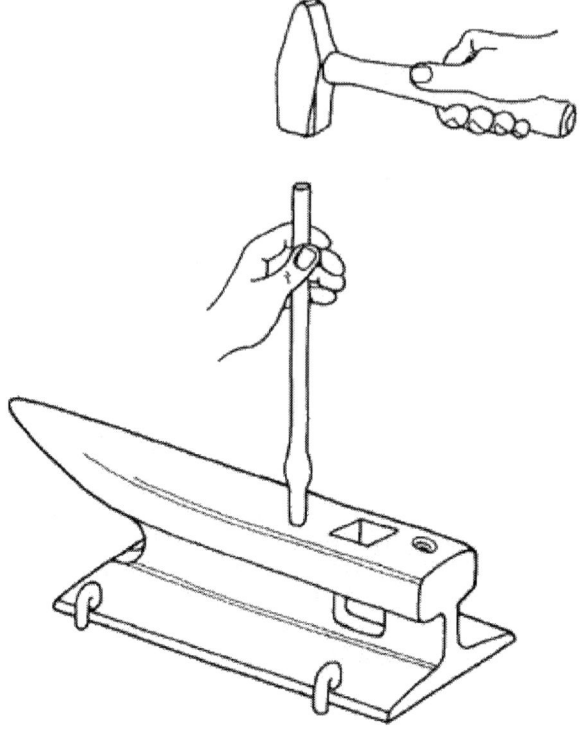

Fig. 4.24

Twisting

Twisting refers to bending one part of the metal laterally while holding another part still.

Twisting a square rod;

Use vice to hold the bottom of the rod in a tight position. Use a spanner to twist the upper part until you get the form you desire.

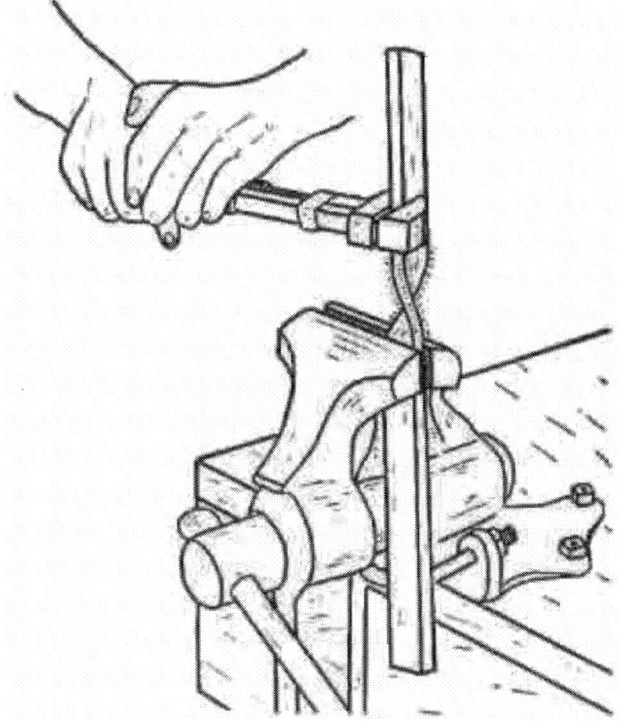

Fig. 4.25

Punching and drifting

Punching is to create a hole into a metal.

Step 1: place the metal on the anvil and use hot or cold eye chisel or drift

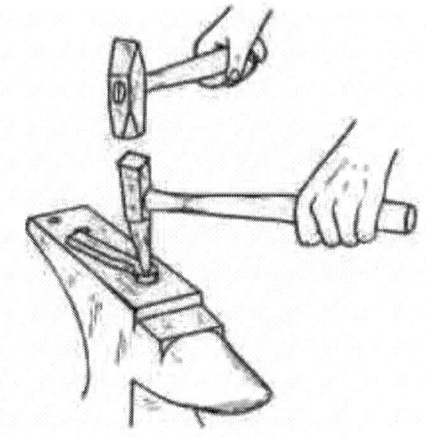

Fig. 4.26

Step 2: hammer until the eye chisel or drift almost reaches the anvil surface

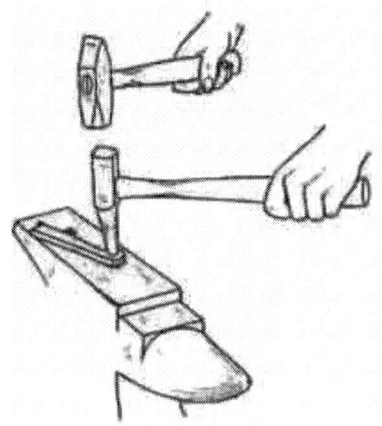

Fig. 4.27

Step 3: reposition the dimpled part to face the anvil hole, position the eye chisel or drift and continue hitting until an eyelet forms through.

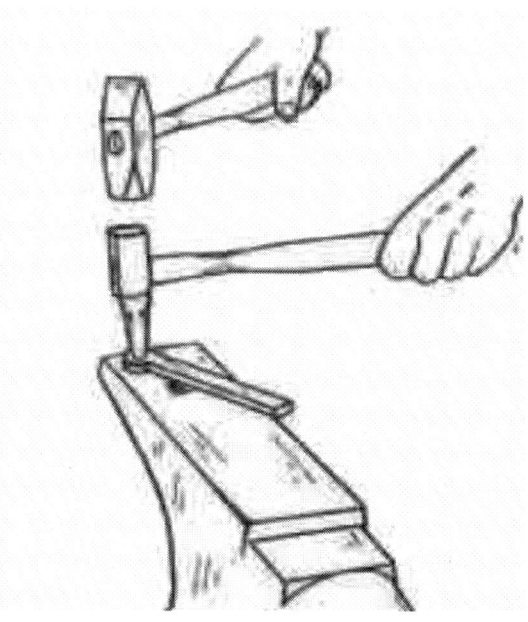

Fig. 4.28

Fire-Welding

Welding two rods

Step 1: forge one end of the first rod and draw it to appear as shown

Fig. 4.29

Step: forge one end of the other rod and draw to appear as shown

Fig. 4.30

Step 3: superimpose one of the drawn edges on the other as shown below and hammer them together

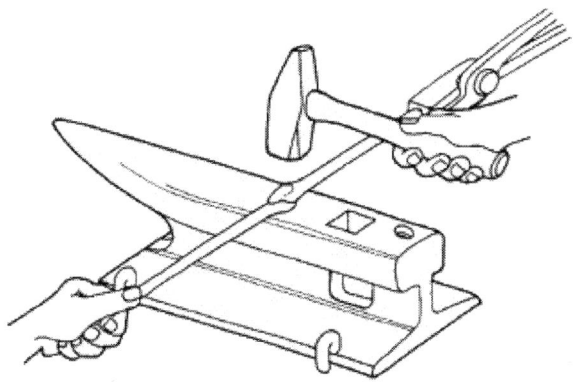

Fig. 4.31

Step 4: continue to hammer until the form a joint as shown below

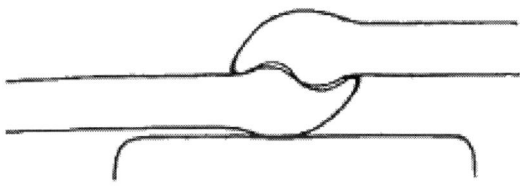

Fig. 4.32

Step 5: hammer evenly till the bulged edges almost disappears as shown below

Fig. 4.33

Tampering

Tampering chisel;

Step 1: dip the pointed chisel part in the tampering agent (water, oil, or other preferred solution.

Fig.4.34

Step 2: quickly remove the chisel while it is still not yet cool and wipe the dipped part with a dry piece of cloth.

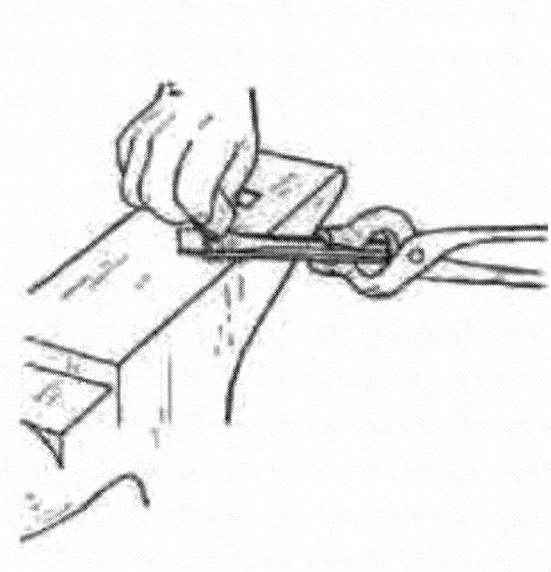

Fig. 4.35

Chapter 5 – Making Your Own Blacksmithing Tools

The great thing with blacksmithing is that you can create your own tools to expand your workshop. If you have the skills, you probably can start off by borrowing the basic tools from a fellow blacksmith and use them to start building your own tools. Sometimes these tools get worn out over time. What a better way to replenish them than make your own? This is the main reason why I really love blacksmithing. How I wish I could do the same with carpentry and masonry.

In this chapter, we will focus on making blacksmith tools. The following are the tools to be made under this project;

Tip;

- Start with small tools as you advance to bigger tools
- Use recyclable materials
- Old vehicle parts collected from vehicle repair workshop can do

Project 1: Round Punch

Raw materials;

- Used vehicle coil spring, torsion spring or anti-roll bars

Tools required;

- Anvil

- Tongs
- Hot set

Instructional steps

Step 1: Draw a chalk line marking the length of the round punch that you want

Step 2: Roll a coil spring along the anvil's face towards the chalk line as shown in the figure below as if you are uncoiling it. This will help you to measure the length that you need to uncoil.

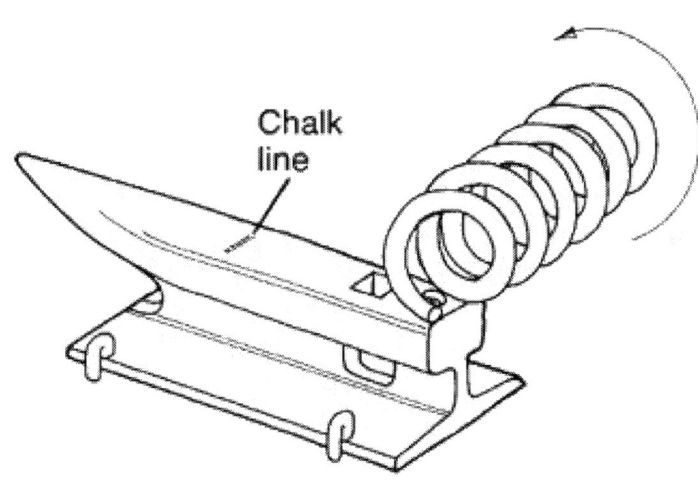

Fig. 5.0

Step 2: Mark the coil at that point touching the chalk line.

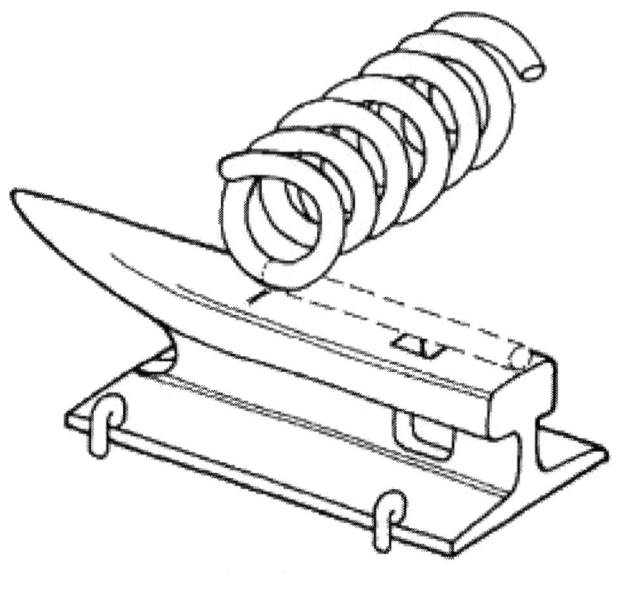

Fig. 5.1

Step 3: Use cold set or hot set (depending on whether you are forging the cut out point or not) to cut the coil at the marked point as shown in figure below

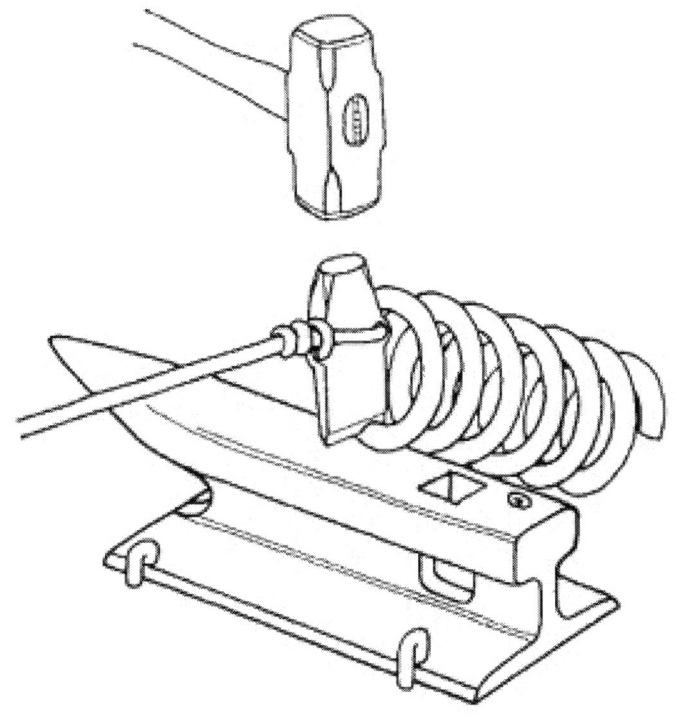

Fig. 5.2

Step 4: straighten the cut out piece of coil for the round punch

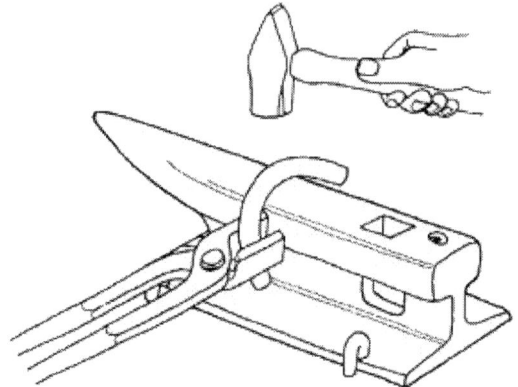

Fig. 5.3 1

Step 5: Point one end of the punch as shown in the figure below

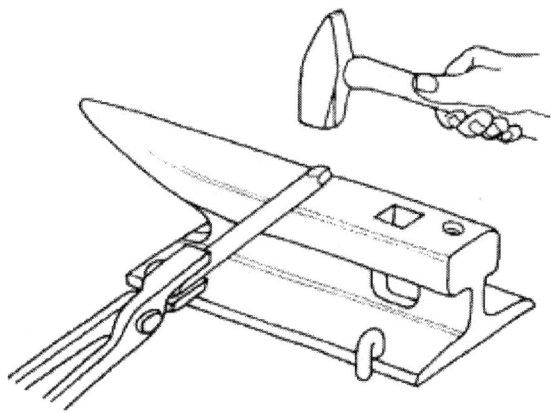

Fig. 5.4

Step 6: hit the pointed end of the punch with a hammer as to flatten it for punching

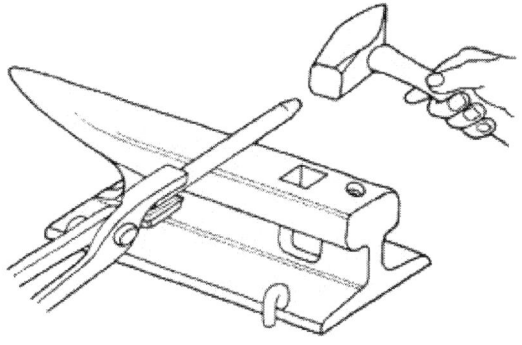

Fig. 5.5

Final piece

Fig. 5.6

Project 2: Hot Chisel

Raw materials;

- Old car half-shaft, torsion bar or anti-roll bars

Tools required;

- Anvil
- Hammer
- Tongs
- Hot set

Instructional steps

Step 1: cut off the unwanted part of the half-shaft as shown below

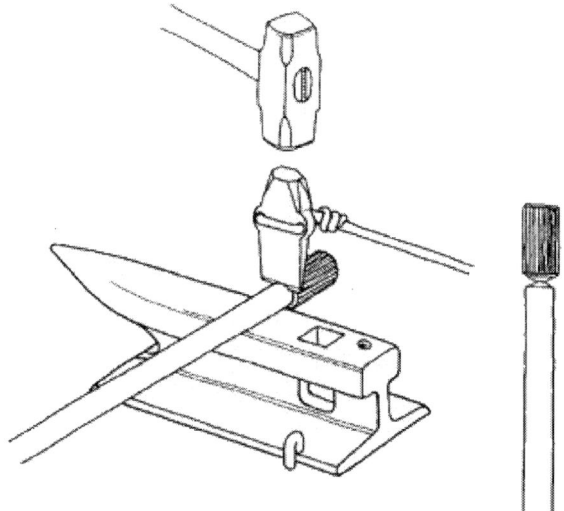

Fig. 5.7

Step 2: cut to required length

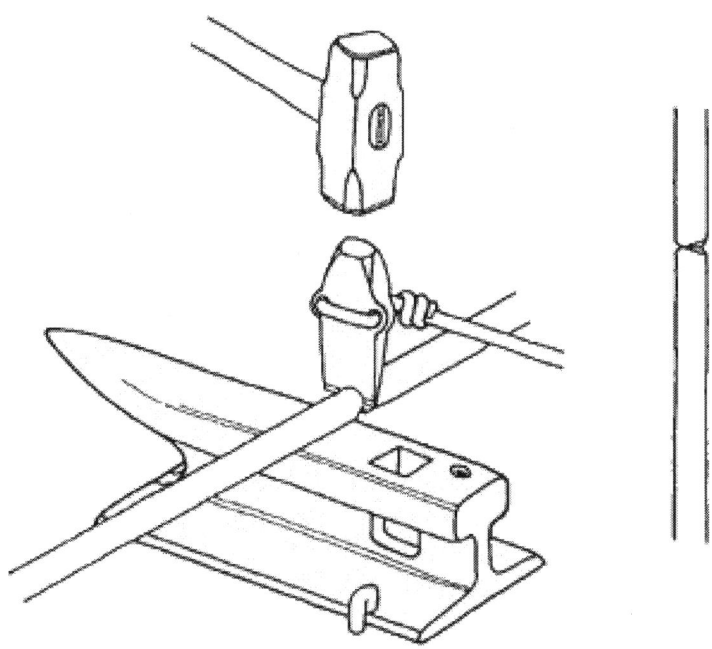

Fig. 5.8

Step 4: draw down one end of the rod so as to have two angular flat sides as shown below

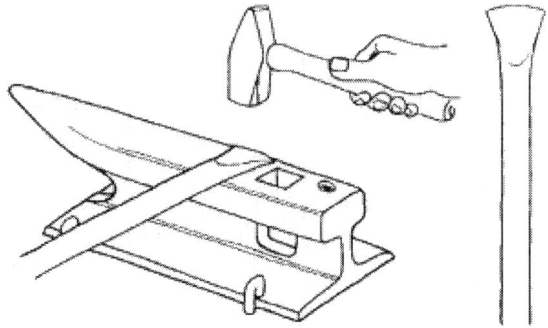

Fig. 5.9

Finished

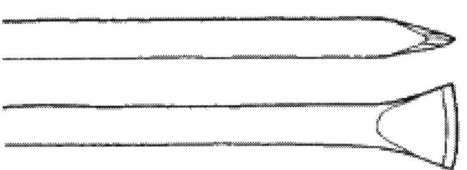

Fig. 5.10

Project 3: Cold Chisel

Raw materials;

- Used vehicle coil spring, torsion spring or anti-roll bars

Tools required;

- Anvil
- Hammer
- Tongs
- Hot set

Instructional steps

Steps 1 to 4 for making round punch

Step 5: draw down one end of the rod so as to have two angular flat sides as shown below

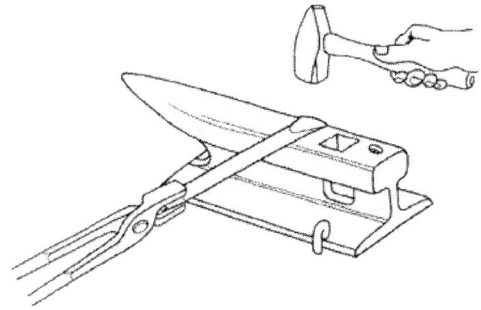

Fig. 5.11

Step 6: lightly hammer the slender sides to make them even

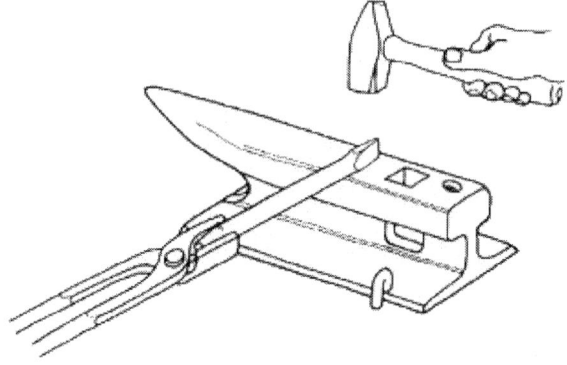

Fig. 5.12

Step 7: Tamper the pointed end by dipping it into the water bucket while still hot

Fig. 5.13

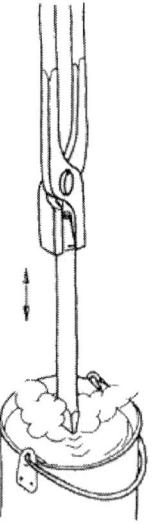

Step 8: remove from the water and wipe off

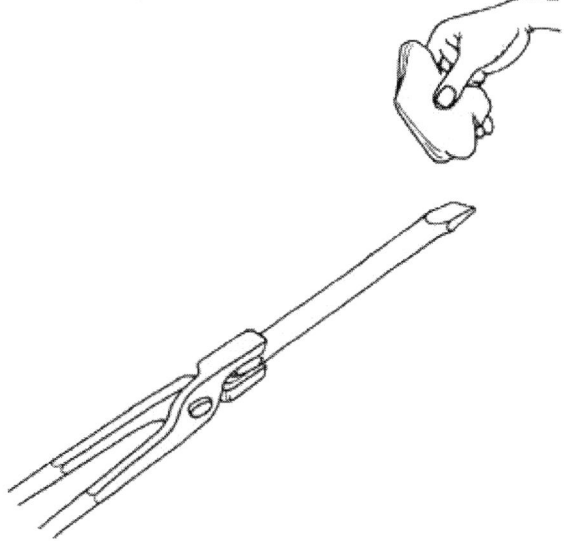

Fig. 5.14

Finished

Fig. 5.15

Project 4: Hot Set

Raw materials;

- Used vehicle leaf spring
- 10mm rounded mild steel (for handle)

Tools required;

- Anvil
- Hammer
- Tongs
- Hot set

Instructional steps

Step 1: cut the required size from the leaf spring

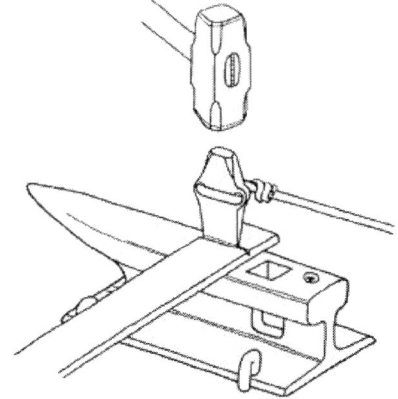

Fig. 5.16

Step 2: push the cut out point to the edge of the anvil letting the cut out part dangling free. Slightly hit it with a hammer to let it fall off

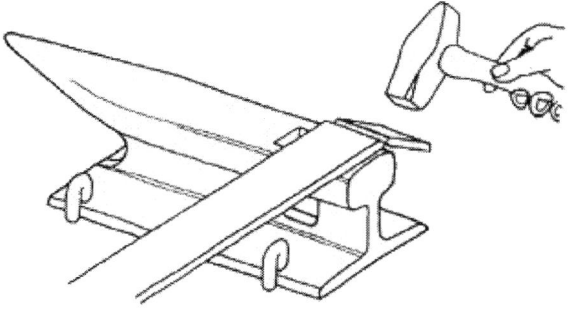

Fig.5.17

Step 3: use tongs to hold the cut out part and draw down to form a flat-chisel point.

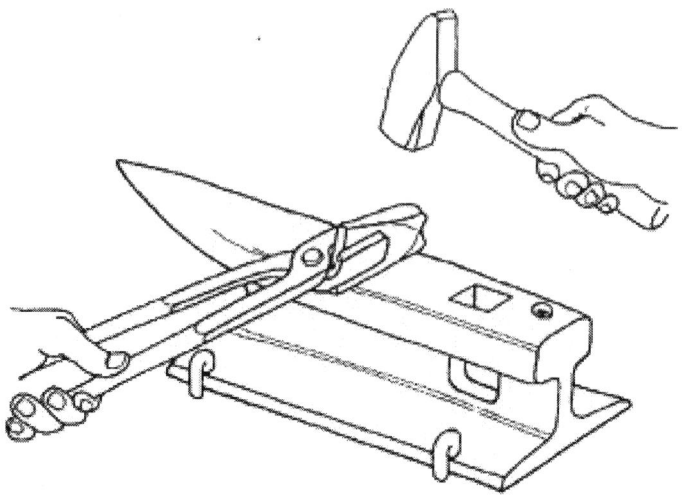

Fig. 5.18

Step 4: lightly hammer the pointed end to make it a bit flat.

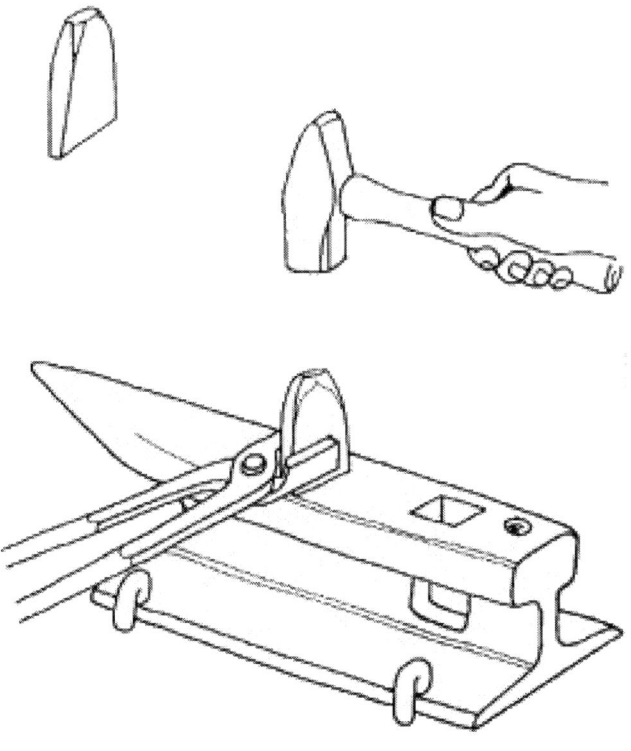

Fig. 5.19

Step 5: punch near the edge of one side to form an eyelet but don't let the round punch reach the anvil as it could damage it or get damaged.

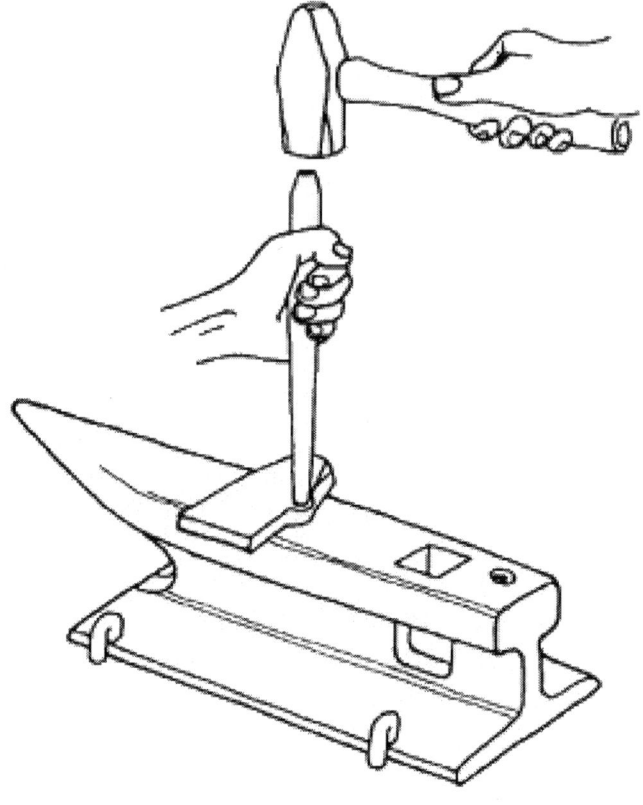

Fig. 5.20

Step 6: turn over to the other side, position the dimpled part to face the anvil hole and punch the same spot on the opposite end to hole through

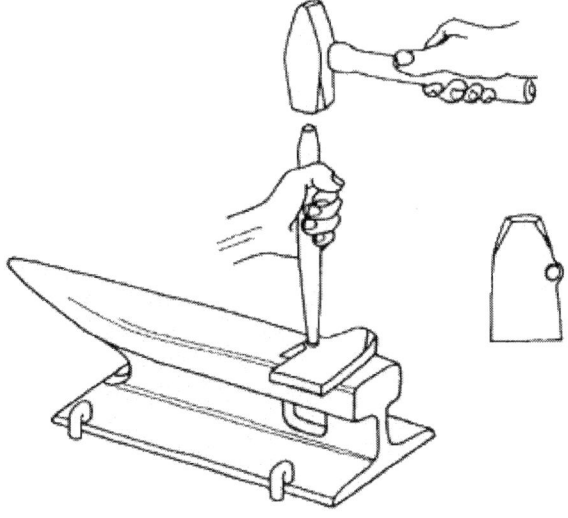

Fig. 5.21

Step 7: test the size of the eyelet to make sure that the rod passes through, if not continue punching and testing until the hole is of the right size.

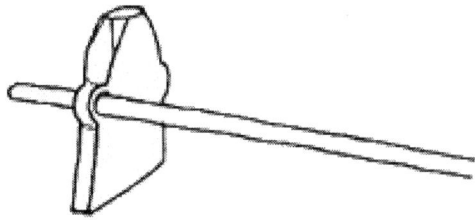

Fig. 5.22

Step 8: repeat the same process on the opposite side of the punched hole

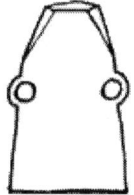

Fig. 5.23

Step 9: draw down further as shown below

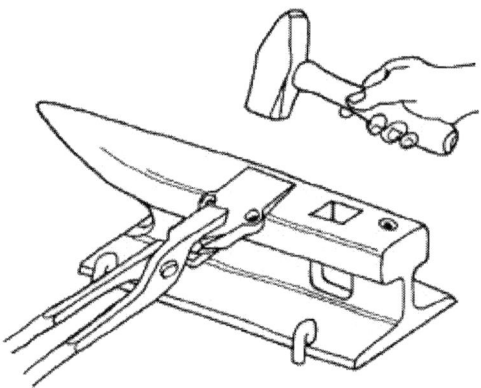

Fig. 5.24

Finished blade of the hot set

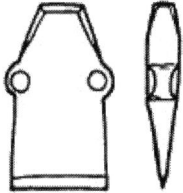

Fig. 5.25

Step 11: Point the rod to be passed through the eyelets to form the handle

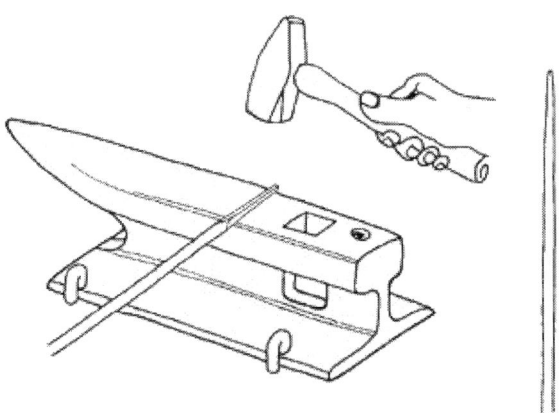

Fig. 5.26

Step 12: bend the rod by hammering it lightly at the edge of the anvil

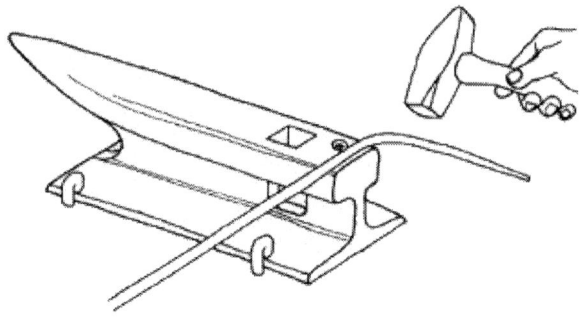

Fig. 5.27

Step 13: bend the rod further to form some kind of a 'U' hook

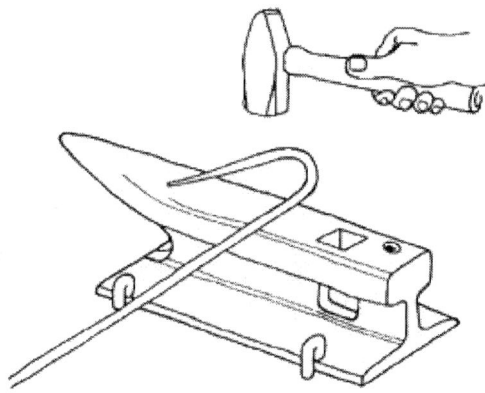

Fig. 5.28

Step 14: insert the hooked part into the eyelets as shown below

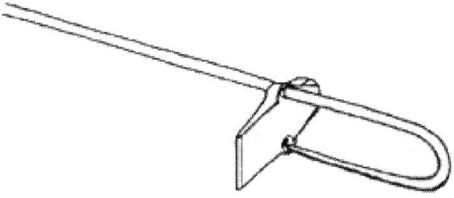

Fig. 5.29

Step 15: hammer the hooked part in further to rest tightly on the hot set blade

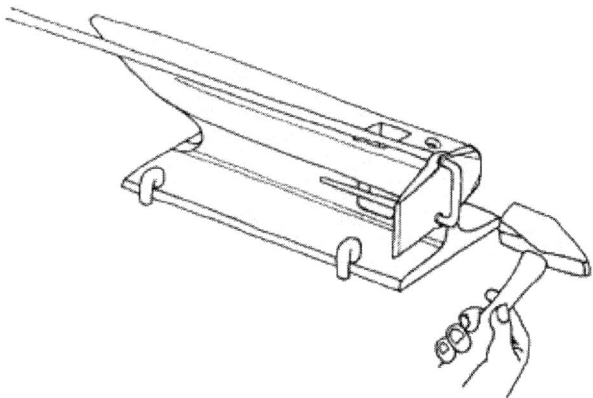

Fig. 5.30

The hooked part properly fitting the hot set blade after hammering

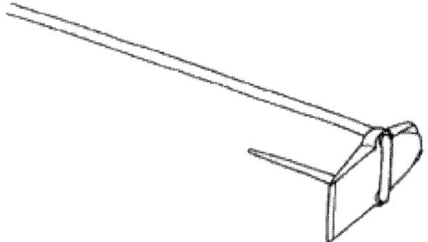

Fig. 5.31

Step 17: bend the two extensions of the rod as shown below

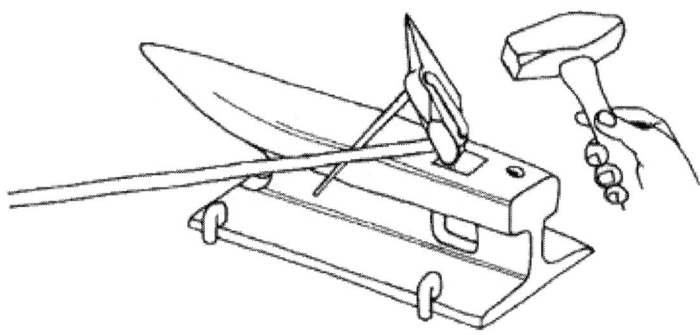

Extensions properly bent to tightly hold the blade

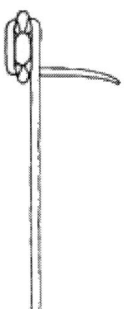

Step 19: hammer the shorter extension (end) of the rod to appear perpendicular to the longer one

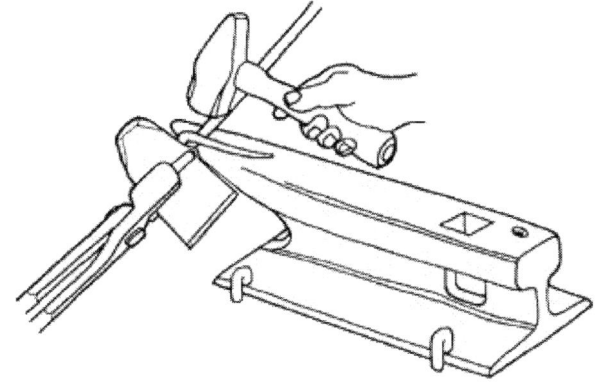

Step 20: Use tongs to properly hold the hot set blade and the longer extension of the rod together as shown below

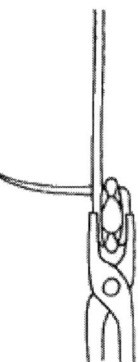

Step 21: hammer to twist the shorter extension around the longer extension to form a handle

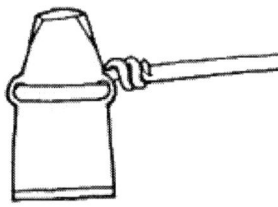

Alternative

Instead of an eyelet, you can create a notch in its place and twist the rod once around the notch leaving two extensions of equal length from the blade to form the handle.

To increase the handling grip, you can create a gap between the two extensions for easy handling using the anvil horn as shown below;

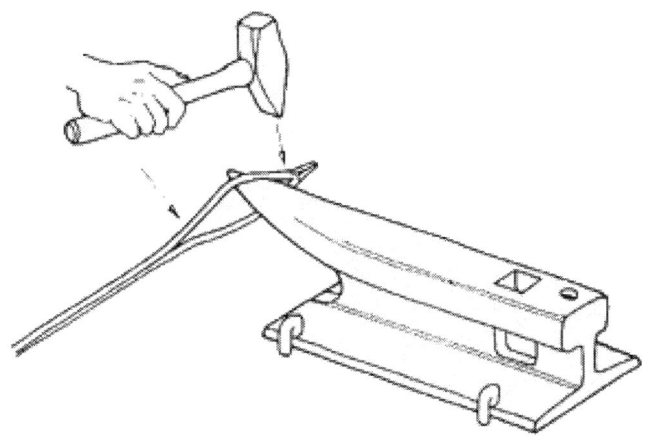

You can then you pliers to twist the ends after the gaps while still in the anvil horn. The twisted end will appear as shown below;

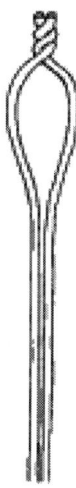

Finished set

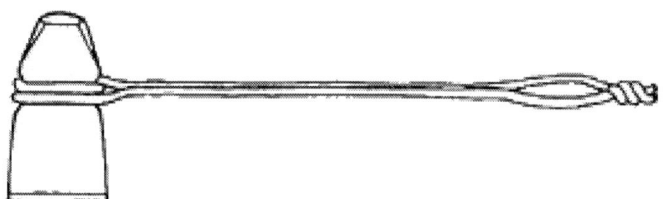

Project 5: Cold Set

Cold set can be made through the same steps as for hot set. However, the blade section should be made thick. The cutting edge should be hardened and tempered.

Project 6: Tongs

Raw materials;

- round mild steel (20mm diameter by 400mm long)

Tools required;

- Anvil
- Hammer
- Tongs
- Hot set

Instructional steps

Step 1 take one end of the round mild steel and place it at the edge of the anvil to draw as shown below;

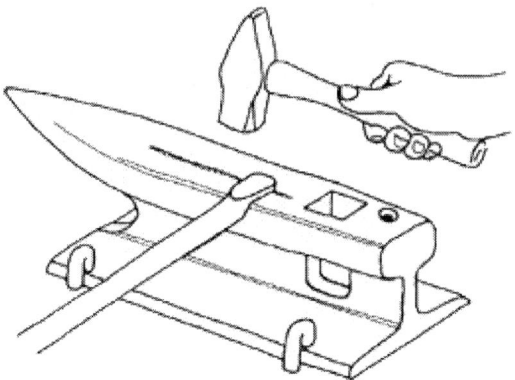

Drawn edge

Step 2: draw to flatten the narrow sides extending slightly further away as shown below

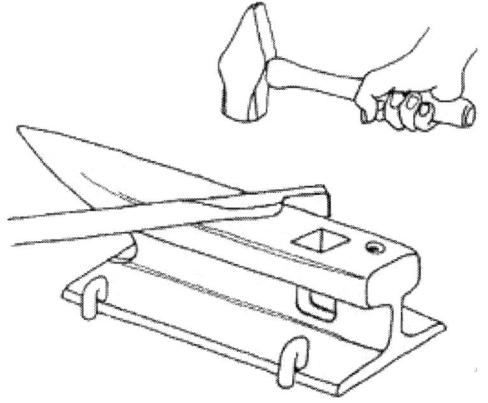

Flattened narrow sides

Step 3: hammer the other two sides opposite the narrow sides beyond the drawn edge as shown below;

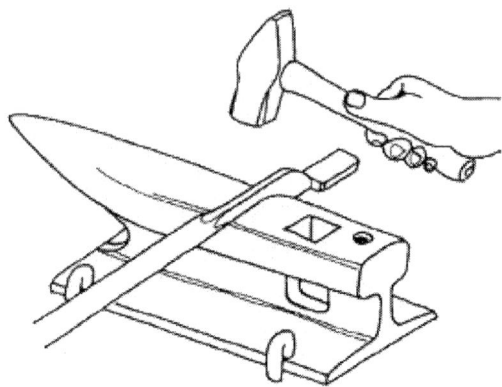

Flattened sides after the drawn edge

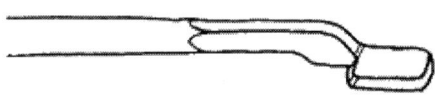

Step 4: Extend the flattening to form the length of the handle as shown below

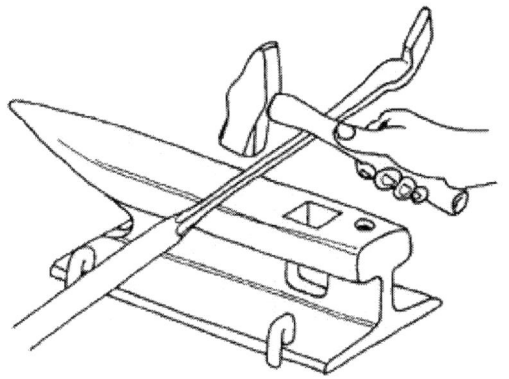

Step 5: cut off the unwanted part of the metal as shown below;

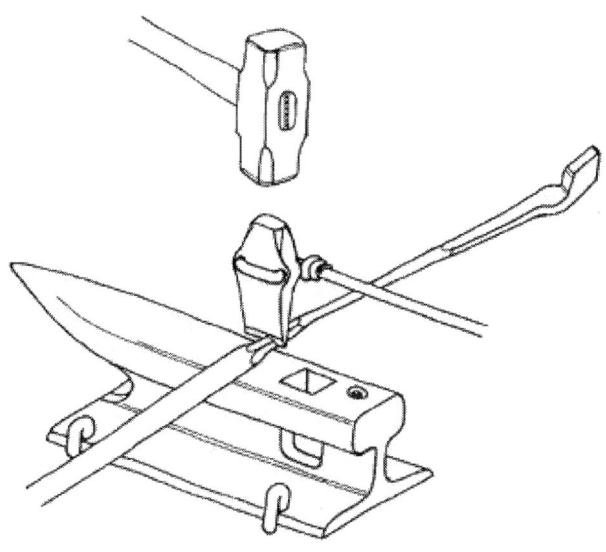

Step 6: Hammer lightly to round the cut out end as shown below;

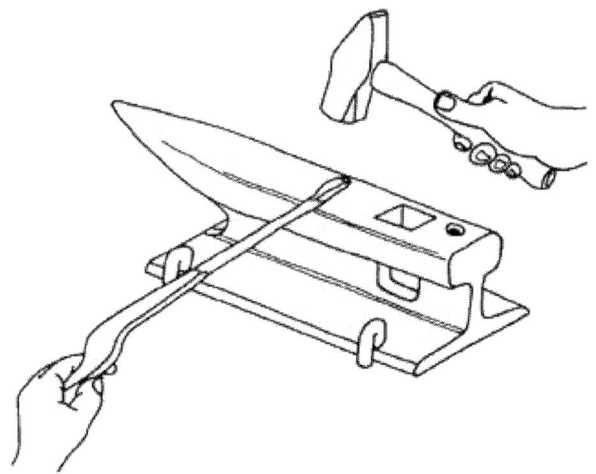

Rounded tail end

Step 7: bend further near the head tip to form a joint which will be screwed to the other pair

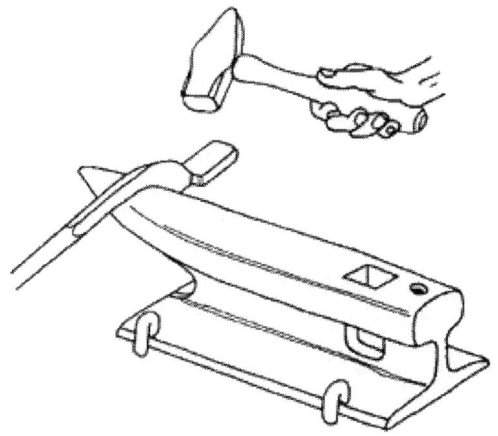

Bent joint

Step 8: punch hole through the side of the head joint as shown below using round punch, but make sure the punch doesn't go through to damage the anvil

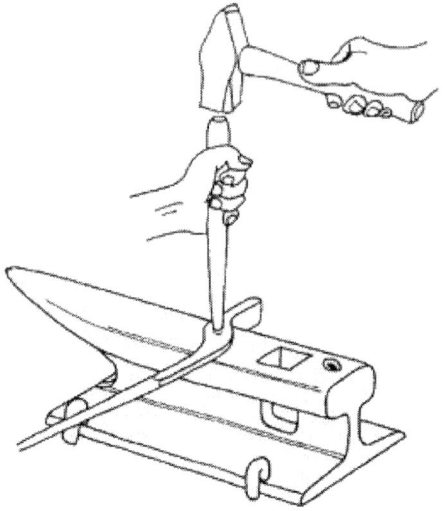

Step 9: turn over so that the dimple faces the anvil hole and punch through the opposite end of it to form an eyelet

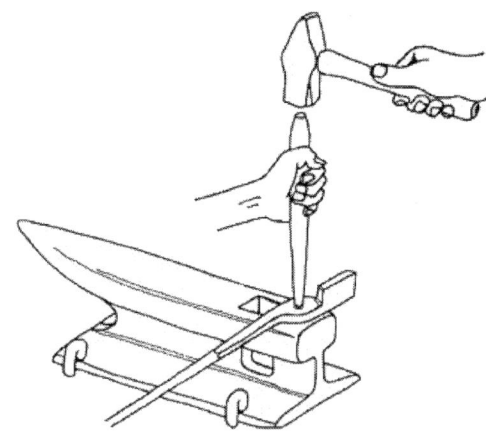

Repeat the steps 1 to 10 for the other pair. The pair will appear as shown below

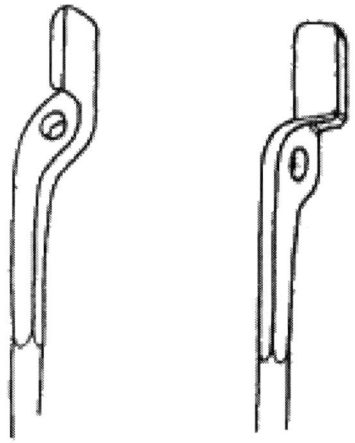

Making the joint rivet

Step 1: point an edge of a rod as shown below. Make sure that its length is enough to penetrate through the eyelets of the two pairs of the tong

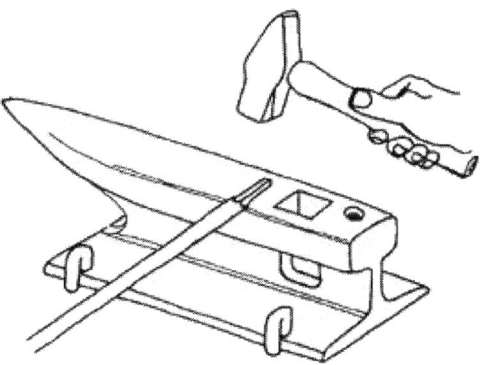

Pointed edge of a rod

Step 2: insert through one half of the pair through to the other as shown below to test the length

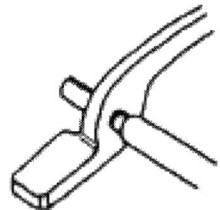

The pointed end through the eyelets of the pair of tongs

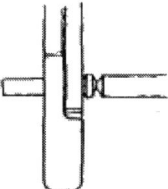

Step 3: draw a ridge around the rod just about a millimeter from the point where the rod had initially been drawn as shown below;

Step 4: re-insert the pointed end into the eyelets as shown below and bend the rod to cut out unwanted part of the rod.

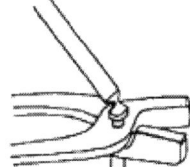

Step 5: place the tongs joint resting on the anvil as shown below and hammer lightly on the rivet to pan it out.

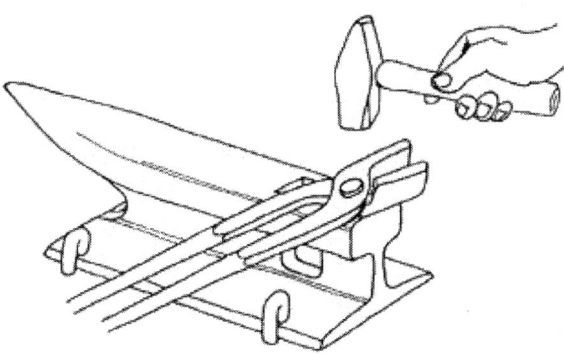

Step 6: turn it over and repeat step 5 on the other end of the rivet

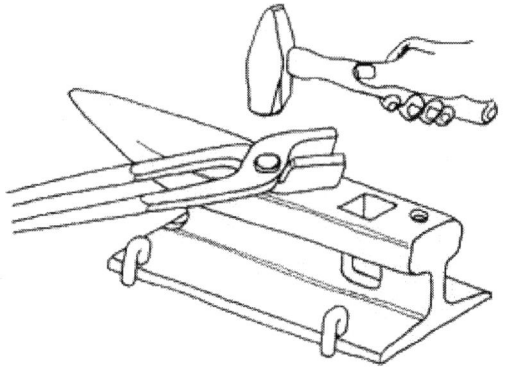

Step 7: forge jaws of the tongs, place a round piece of rod between them and hammer lightly as shown below;

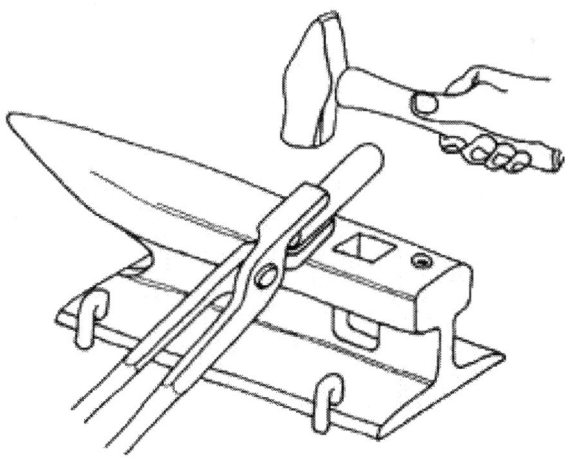

Rounded jaws

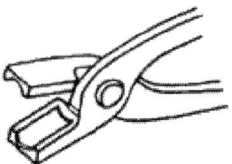

Step 8: place a rounded piece of metal in between the handles of the tongs and a piece from leaf spring into the jaws, quench the tongs in water as you close and open the jaws to ensure that they can open and close.

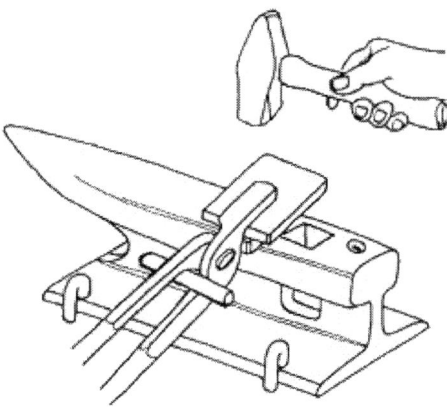

Finished tongs

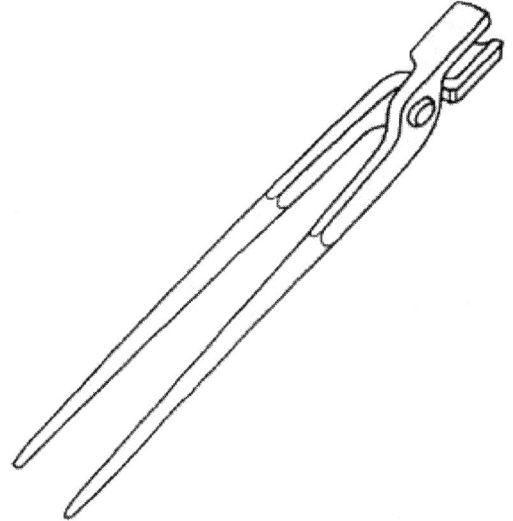

Project 7: Fullers

Raw materials;

- Mild steel rod

Tools required;

- Anvil

- Hammer
- Tongs
- Hot set
-

Instructional steps

Step 1: cut two pieces of mild steel rods of the desired length – one for top fuller and the other one for bottom fuller.

Step 2: bend one piece into a 'Z' shape except with right angles as shown below for bottom fuller

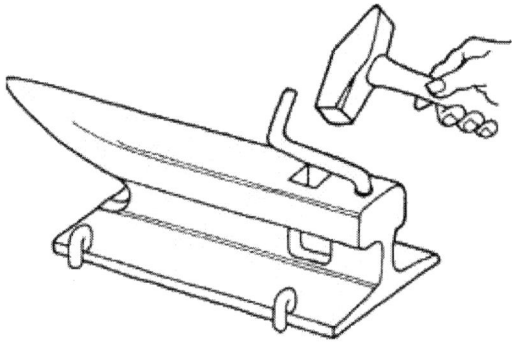

Z-shaped bottom fuller

Leave the other piece as it is to act as the top fuller.

Both bottom fuller and top fuller being used to create grove on the rod

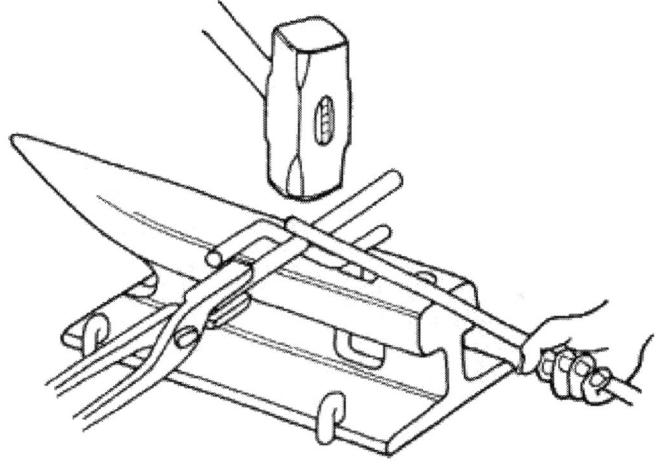

Project 8: Eye Chisel

Raw materials;

- 20-30mm diameter Medium to high carbon steel, at least 400mm long for the handle
- Straightened piece of heavy round coil can also do

Tools required;

- Anvil
- Hammer
- Tongs
- Hot set

Instructional steps

Follow steps 1 to 5 of making a cold chisel

Step 6: continue drawing till all the sides of the pointed end becomes nearly equal and the points become sharper as shown below

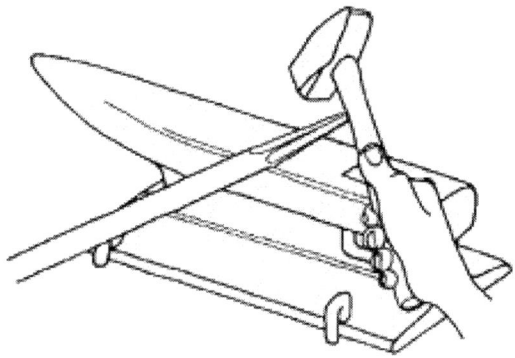

Finished eye chisel

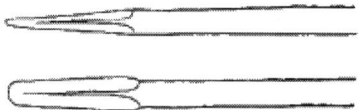

Project 9: Eye Drift

Raw materials;

- Vehicle half-shaft

Tools required;

- Anvil
- Hammer
- Tongs
- Hot set

Instructional steps

Follow steps 1 to 4 for making hot chisel

Step 5 Draw to elongate the pointed end of the eye drift as shown below;

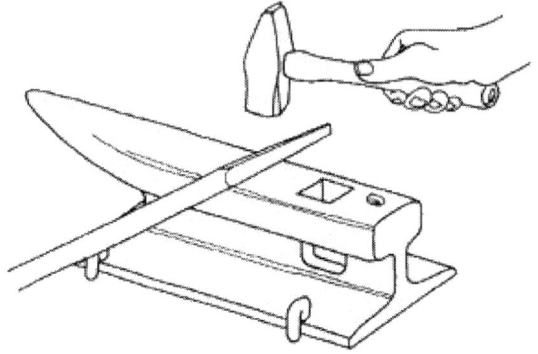

Sides of a finished eye drift

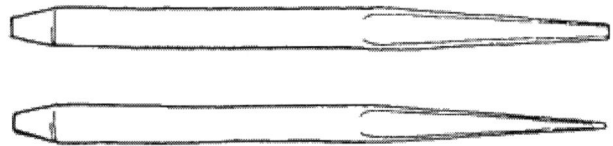

Project 10: Cross Peen Hammer

Raw materials;

- Old vehicle half shaft

Tools required;

- Anvil
- Hammer

- Tongs
- Hot set
- Eye chisel
- Eye drift

Instructional steps

Follow steps 1 and 2 for making hot chisel.

Step 3: draw one end using hammer to make a blunt point as shown below

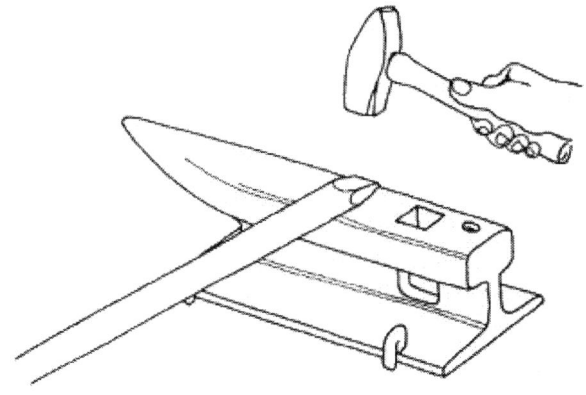

Step 4: trim a thin strip off the pointed edge so as to cut off irregular portion

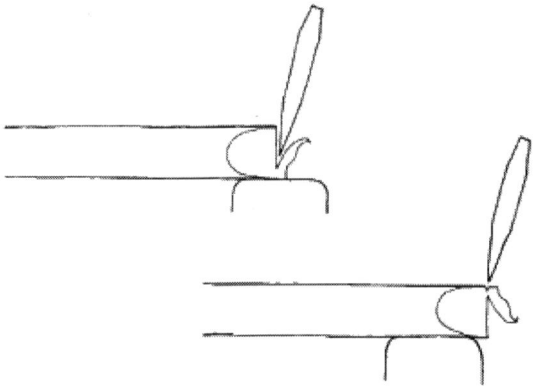

Step 5: hammer the pointed edge after trimming to even out the surface

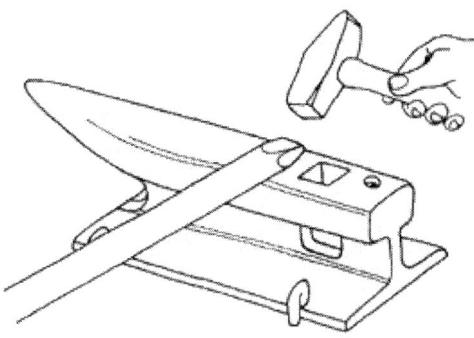

Step 6: just a millimeters away from the pointed edge, hammer to draw a flat surface from which an eyelet can be created for inserting the handle

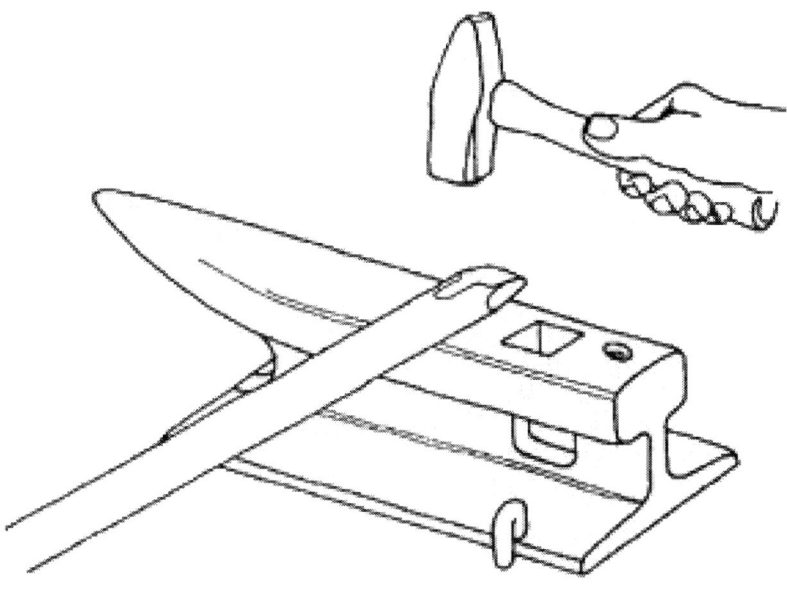

Step 7: use eye chisel to dig up the eye. Make sure that the eye chisel does not pierce through as it could reach and damage the face of the anvil

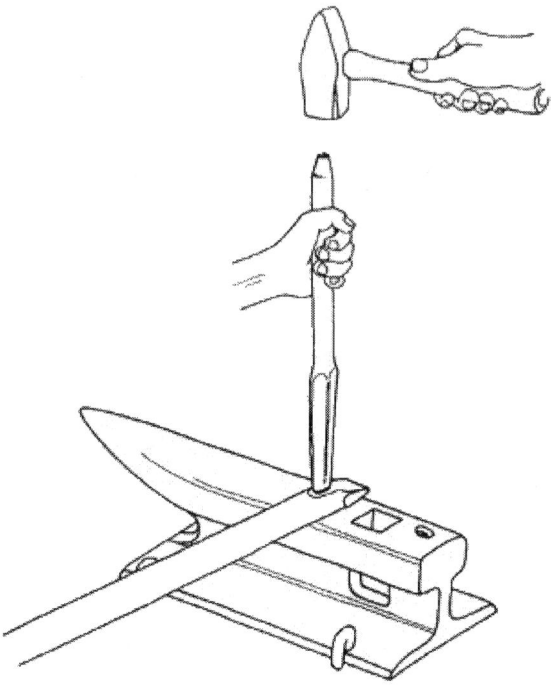

Step 8: turn over such that the dimpled part faces the anvil hole and use the eye chisel to continue punching the eyelet until through

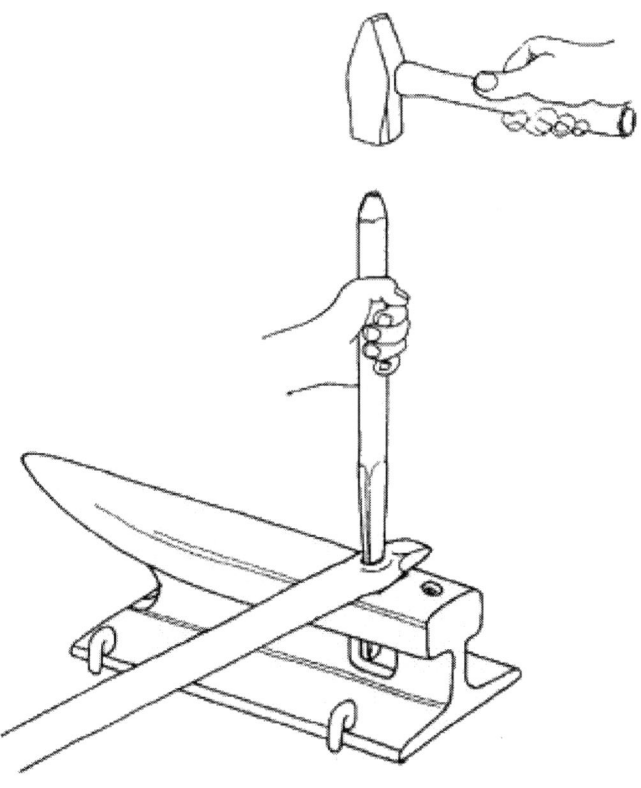

Step 9: Once the eye chisel has pierced through, remove it and hammer the drift through until the size of the eyelet is large enough for the pin of the hammer.

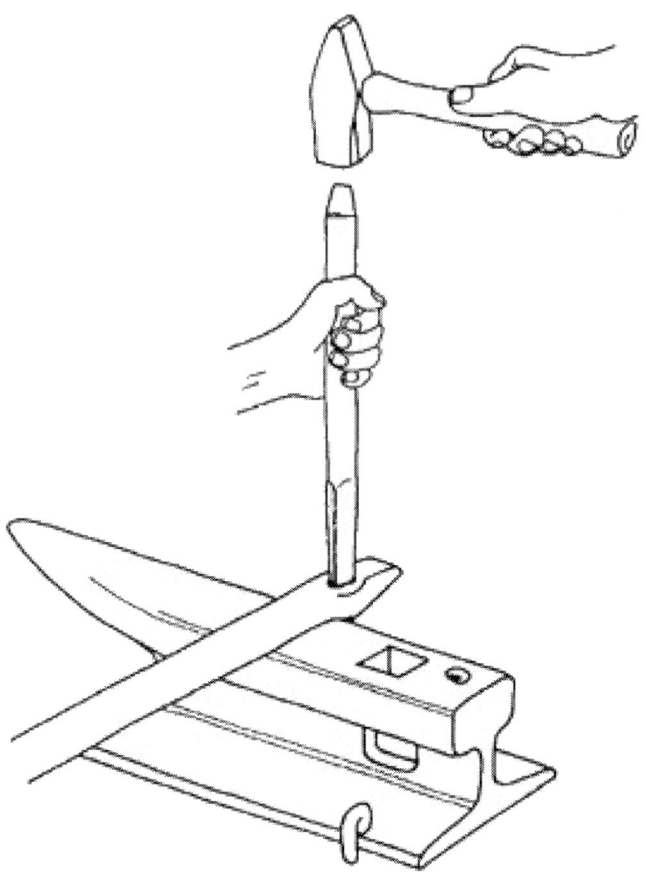

Step 10: lay the shaft across the anvil with the drift inside hammer around the edge of eyelet meeting the drift to form some fatty flesh around.

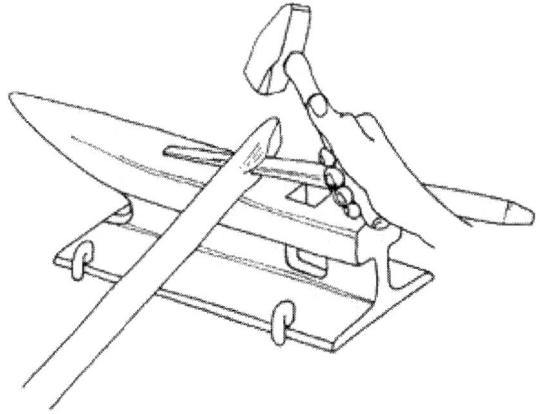

Step 11: Remove the drift and enter it through the other end of the eyelet and repeat step 10 so that both ends of the eyelet will have some thick fatty lips around as shown below;

Step 12: Draw the sides of the eyelet to flatten them as shown below;

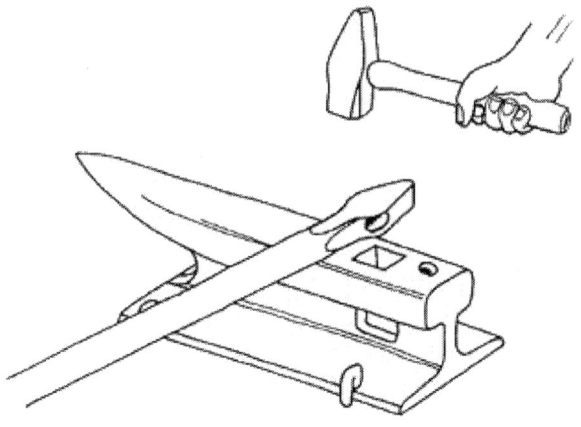

Step 13 Cut out the head of the hammer from the shaft as shown below;

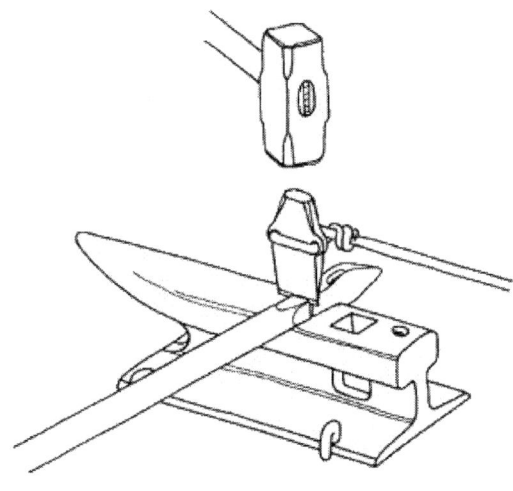

Sides of the cut out hammer head;

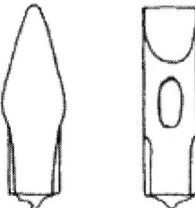

Step 14: trim the edge of the opposite end to the pin to have a flat surface

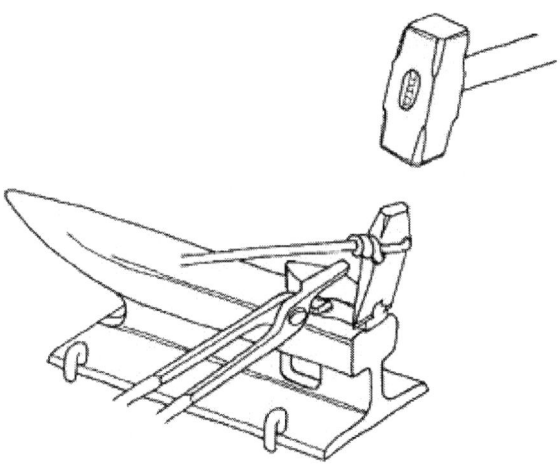

Step 15 use tongs to hold the hammer head with the peen resting onto a trunk of wood. Continue hammering as shown below to widen and flatten the base.

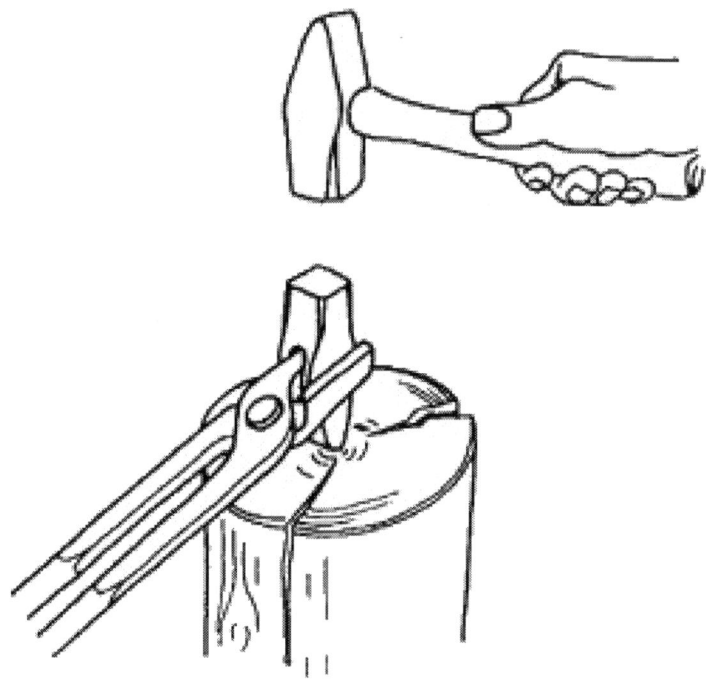

The head is now ready for annealing, hardening and tampering

Step 16: Fix the hammer shaft.

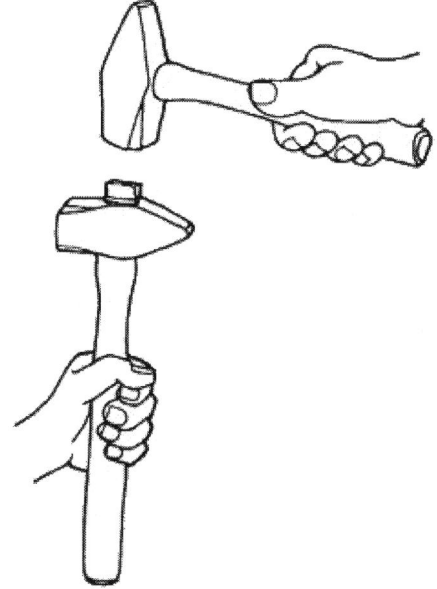

Finished Ball peen hammer

Project 11: Ball Peen Hammer

Raw materials;

- Old vehicle half shaft

Tools required;

- Anvil
- Hammer
- Tongs
- Hot set
- Eye chisel
- Eye drift

Instructional steps

Follow steps 1 and 2 of making ball peen hammer

Step 3: draw multiple-edged blunt point on one end of the shaft as shown below;

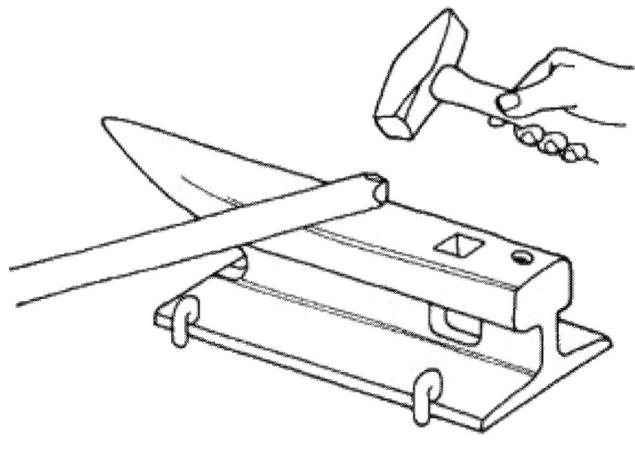

Multiple-edged blunt point;

Step 4: use fullers to draw a groove round the shaft a few millimeters from the drawn multiple edges.

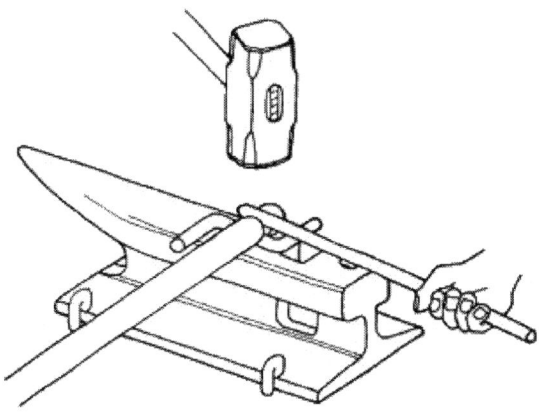

Ball peen created by use of fullers;

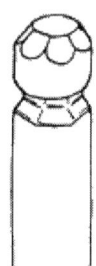

Step 5: continue to lightly hammer around the multiple edges of the ball peen to neutralize the angles and make it round

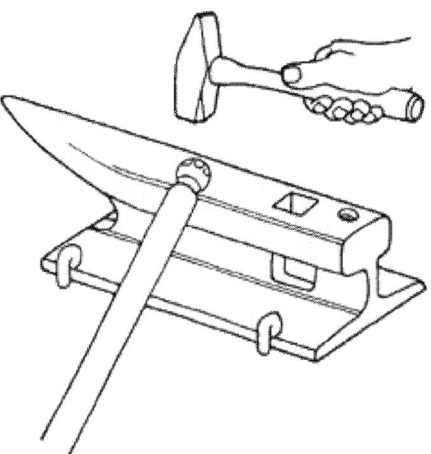

Rounded ball peen;

Step 6: follow steps 7 to 16 of cross peen hammer to form the eyelet, the flat side of the hammer, anneal, tamper and harden the head and to fix the handle.

Finished ball peen hammer;

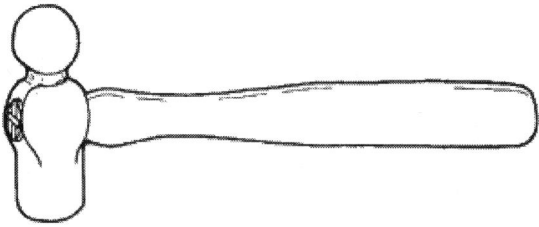

Project 12: Claw Hammer

Raw materials;

- Old vehicle half shaft

Tools required;

- Anvil
- Hammer
- Tongs
- Hot set
- Eye chisel
- Eye drift

Instructional steps

Follow steps 1 and 2 for the ball peen hammer

Preparing the claw:

Step 3: forge one end of the shaft and rest its edge some few millimeters on the anvil and draw down as shown below;

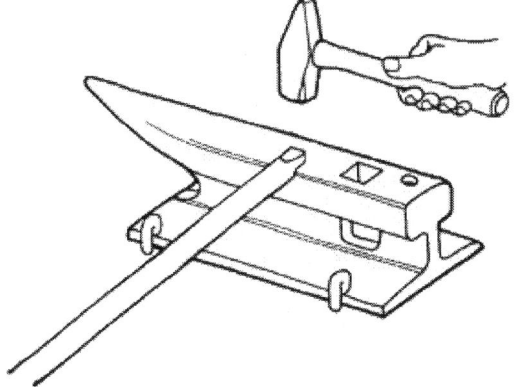

The end will look like this;

Step 2: Continue to hammer to extend the claw part until it is long enough

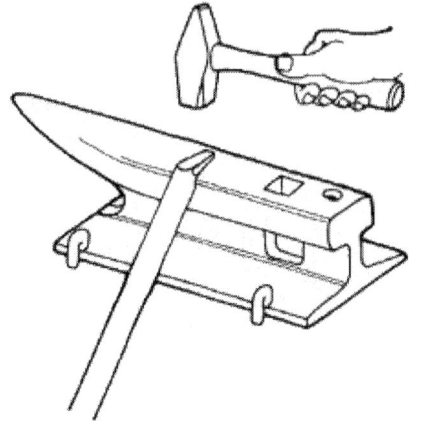

Elongated claw section;

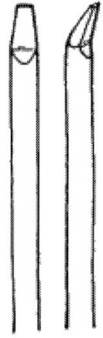

Step 3: rest the claw section onto the anvil as shown below and use hot chisel to dissect the section into two to form a pair of claws;

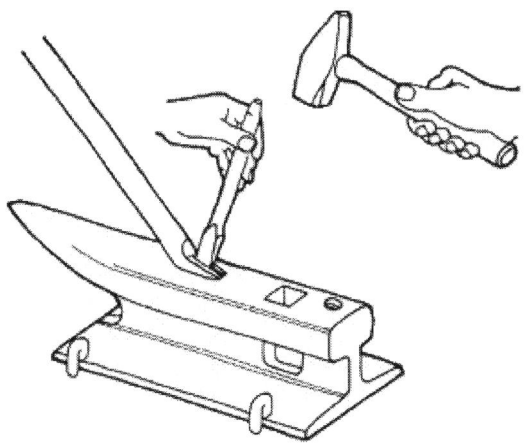

Pair of claws formed;

Step 4: rest a piece of mild steel on the face of the anvil to protect it from piercing hot chisel so that you can completely split in between the pair of claws;

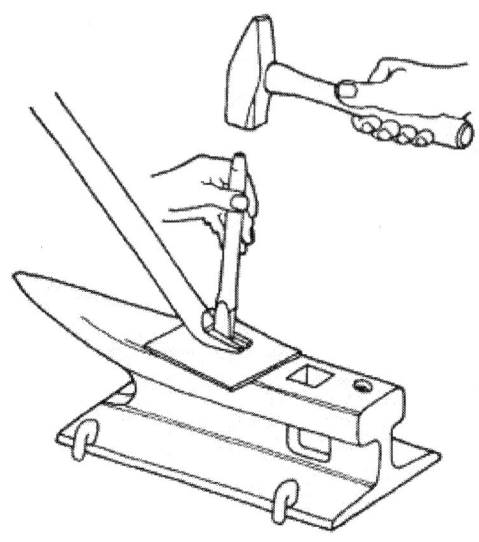

A pair of claws with a complete gap in between;

Step 5: open out the claws of the hammer gently using hot set as shown below;

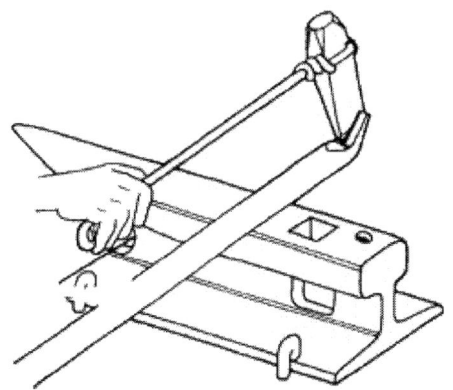

Widened opening of the claws;

Step 6: follow steps 7 to 16 of ball peen hammer to form the eyelet, the flat side of the hammer, anneal, tamper and harden the head and to fix the handle.

Finished claw hammer;

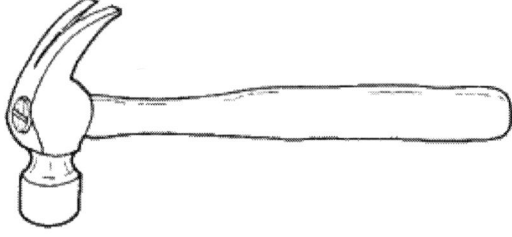

Project 13: Anvil

Raw materials;

- Old rail part

Tools required;

- Anvil
- Hammer
- Tongs
- Hot set
- Eye chisel
- Eye drift

Instructional steps

Step 1: cut a piece of old rail part

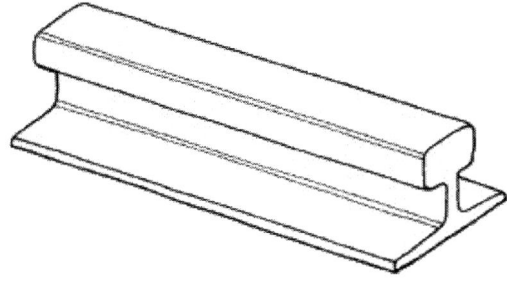

Step 2: mark on the sides of the cut piece of old rail part as shown below

Step 3: mark on top of the piece of old rail part as shown below

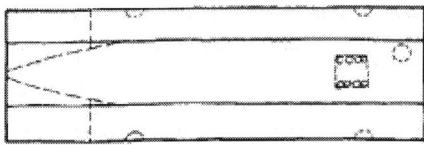

Step 4: forge and cut along the markings shown in step 2 above as shown below

Step 5: forge and cut along the markings shown in step 3 above as shown below and punch the necessary holes too plus including the square hole and round hole on top plus holes the four side notches for anchoring the anvil

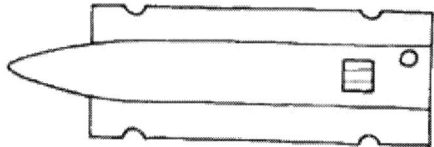

Step 6: finish up the anvil to appear as shown below

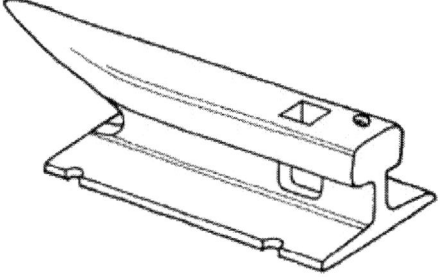

Chapter 6 – Making Your Own Carpentry tools

Carpentry is one of blacksmith's most complementary professions. Having skills in carpentry can be a big plus for your blacksmithing endeavors. Most of the blacksmithing project tools will require wooden handles and frames. With carpentry skills you can easily make them yourself rather than taking to a carpenter.

This chapter provides you with blacksmithing skills required to make essential carpentry tools.

Project 14: Chisel

Raw materials;

- Used leaf spring

Tools required;

- Anvil
- Hammer
- Tongs
- Hot set

Instructional steps

Step 1: cut the leaf spring as per the indicated dimensions below;

Step 2: mark dimensions for cutting and drawing as shown below

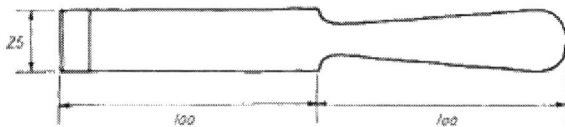

Step 3: use fullers to make groove diving the handle and the blade as shown below;

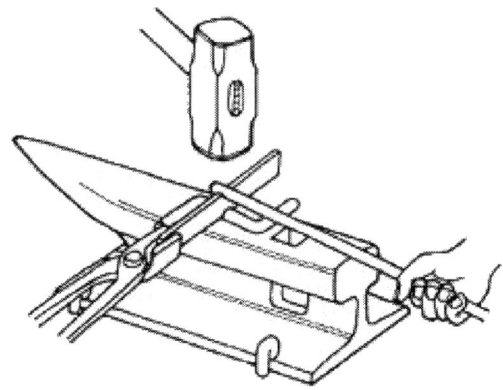

Groove done;

Step 4: place the groove point against the edge of the anvil as shown below and draw to form an even slant of the blade on both sides towards the notch

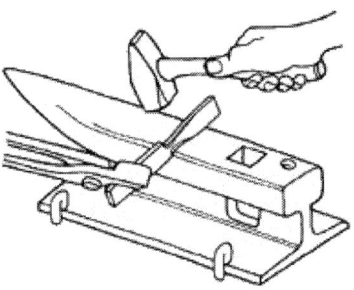

Step 5: draw to flatten the broad sides of the blade

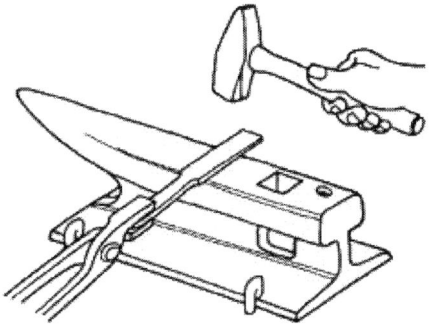

Step 6: hammer the blade on the narrow sides to even out as shown below;

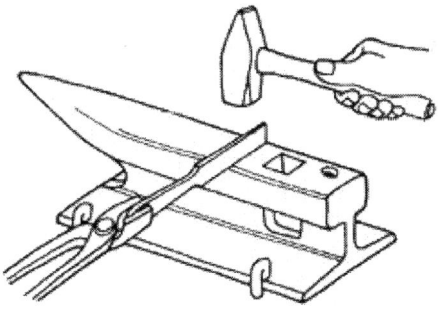

Step 7: hammer the piercing end of the chisel to even out and create on it a slanting edge as shown below;

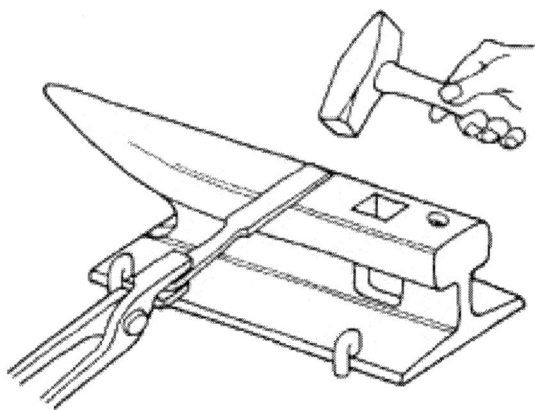

Chisel with evened out sides and a slanting piercing edge

Finished chisel

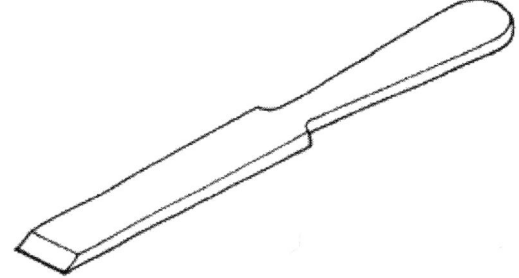

Project 15: Plane Iron

Raw materials;

- Used leaf spring

Tools required;

- Anvil
- Hammer
- Tongs
- Hot set

Instructional steps

Step 1: mark out the leaf spring as shown below;

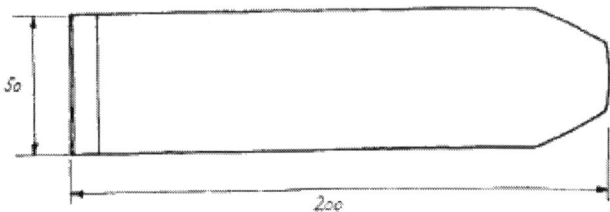

Step 2: Cut the needed part so that it can be forged and cut to dimensions

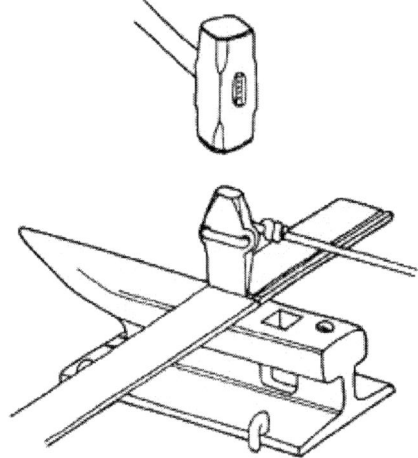

Step 3: cut off the angles on one end of the leaf as per the marked dimensions;

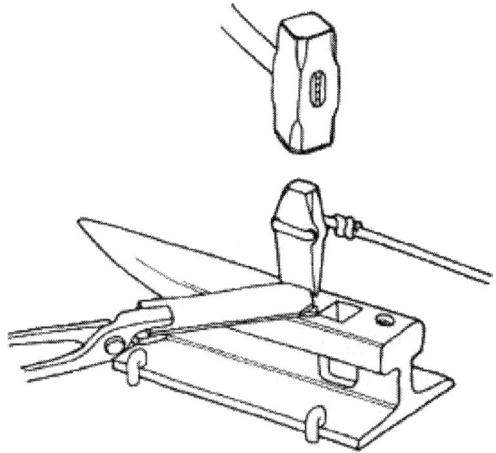

The piece of iron after right angles are cut out;

Step 4: position the opposite end of the cut out angles against the edge of the anvil and draw down at an angle as shown below to create a slanting edge

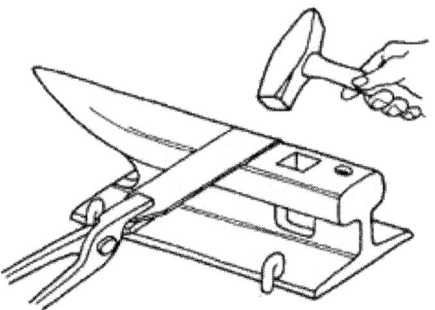

Finished plane iron with a slanting edge;

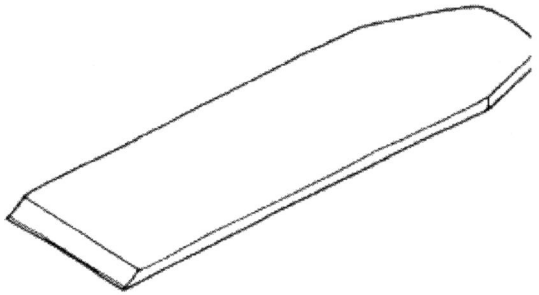

Project 16: Brace

Raw materials;

- Straightened-up coils spring

Tools required;

- Anvil
- Hammer
- Tongs
- Hot set
- Square punch

Instructional steps

Step 1: cut a rod of 60mm long and upset one end

Upsetting one end

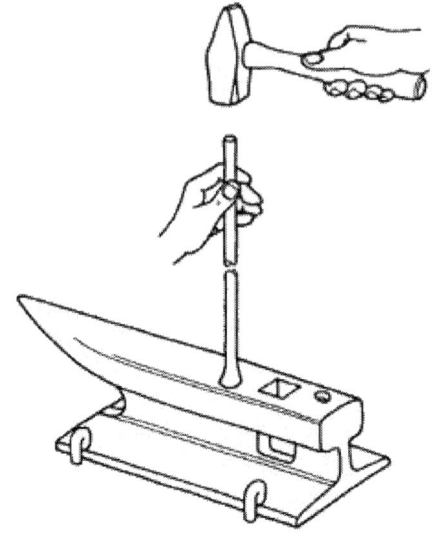

Upset end

Step 2: chamfer the upset end and continue to upset until the width of the upset end reaches 20mm

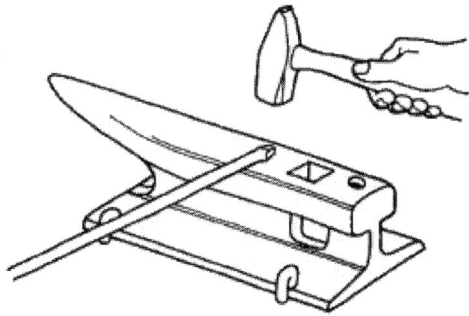

Upset end now chamfered

Step 3: Rest the upset end on the anvil and draw it to flatten the sides till the thickness of the flattened sides equals that of the rest of the rounded body

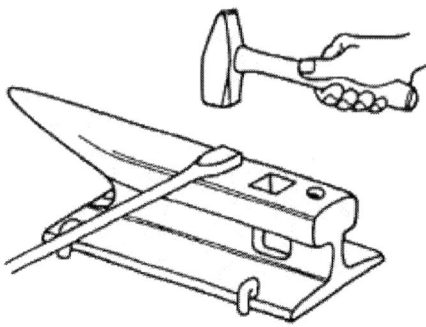

Chamfered end now flattened

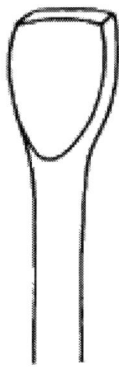

Step 4: use square punch to make a square hole in the middle of the flattened part

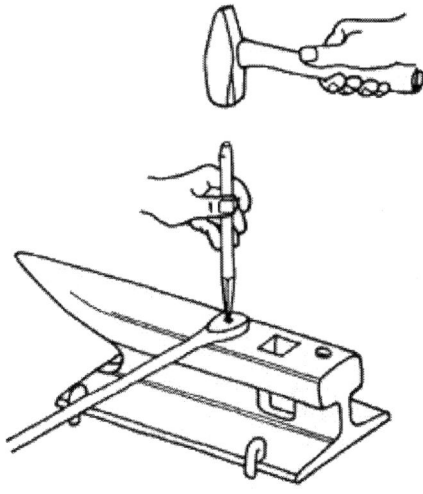

Square hole made

Step 5: mark two points from the edge of the inner border of the punched hole towards the rest of the body the first part (towards the hole) should be 120mm while the next part should be 160mm.

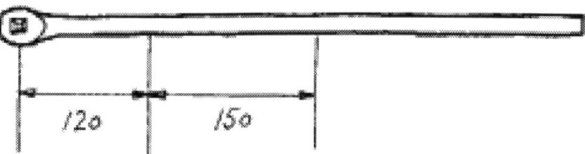

Step 6: forge the border of the two parts and bend at right angle in such a way that the square hole aligns parallel to the main unbend body.

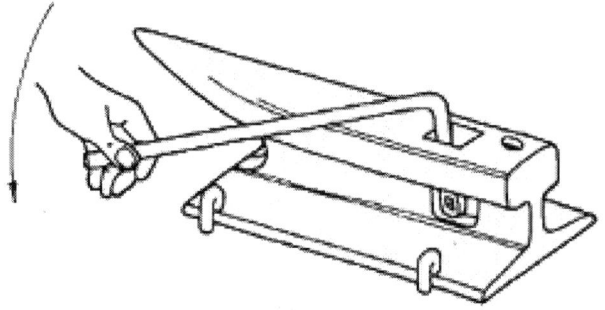

Step 7: bend again at the end of the second portion so that the remaining unbend part runs parallel in the same direction as the part that has the square hole.

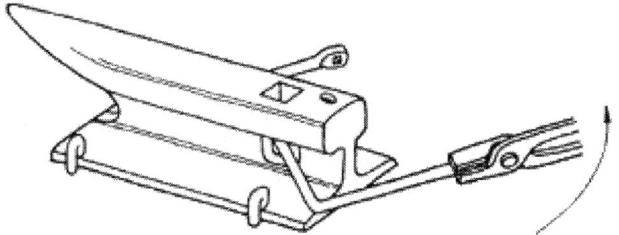

Step 8: bend the remaining part such that the remaining part's angle (the last angle) alights with the square hole and runs parallel to the 150mm portion (portion immediately after the first bend).

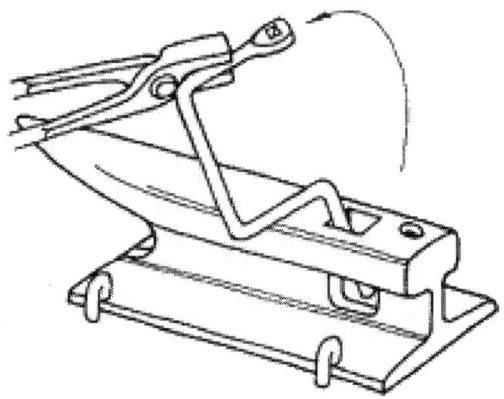

Step 9: you can now fit the wooden handle in the carpentry workshop.

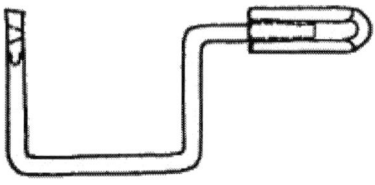

Finished carpenter's brace

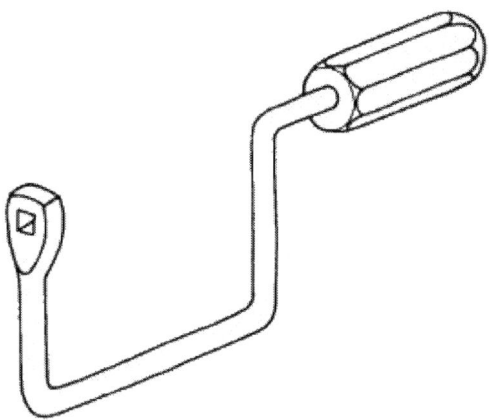

Project 17: Center Bit

Raw materials;

- Used vehicle coil spring - straighten out a coil measuring 100mm long and 12mm diameter

Tools required;

- Anvil
- Hammer
- Tongs
- Hot set

Instructional steps

Follow steps 1 to 6 for making a cold chisel except that the straighten out coil will be measuring 100mm long and 12mm diameter

Step 7: mark 40mm on one end that will be square pointed to fit into the square hole of the brace. Mark 20mm from the opposite end for the center tooth. This will be the length of the center tooth. Mark 15mm from the end of the 20mm (center tooth) measurement towards the edge where the 20mm begins. This will be the length of the two end teeth.

Step 8: mark two points on the baseline such as to divide the 20mm width of the flattened edge into three equal sections.

Step 9: cut from the center of the flattened edge towards the two points in step 3. This will form a saw tooth in the center and two other saw teeth each to the left and right as shown below.

Step 10: test to fit the bit into the brace you made

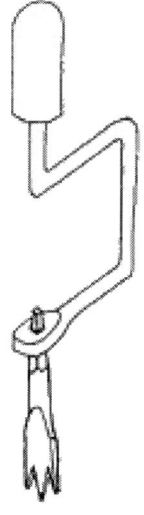

Chapter 7 - Making Common Home Tools Using Your Own Created Tools

Beyond workshop environment, you need to make products for non-workshop application, more so, for your own home use or for others to use in their homes.

This chapter introduces the most common yet basic home tools that you can start off making as part of your blacksmithing endeavor.

Project 18: Knife

Raw materials;

- High carbon steel.
- Used thin leaf spring can be used instead.

Tools required;

- Anvil
- Hammer
- Tongs
- Hot set
- Eye chisel

- Eye drift

Instructional steps

Step 1: cut a piece of leaf spring long enough for the size of knife that you want

Step 2: mark the length into three equal parts. Mark to divide the last part it into two lengthwise as shown in the diagram.

Step 3: forge and cut off half the length of the last third that you have marked using hot set to form the handle part.

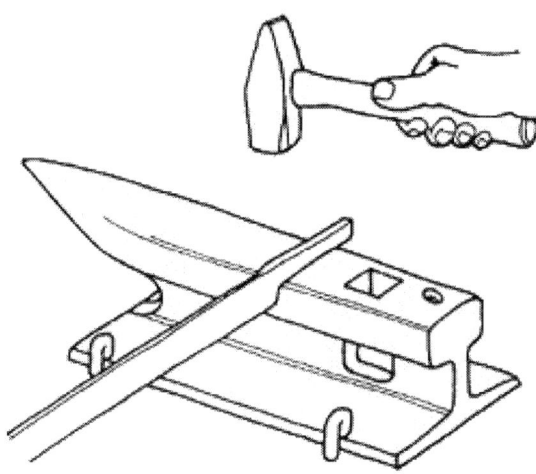

Step 4: hammer the sides of the handle until they get a fat and thicker shape

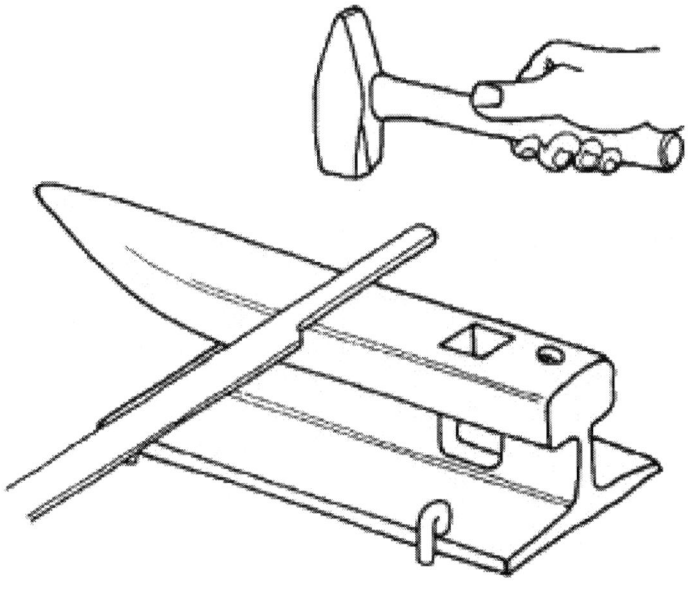

Step 5: cut an edge of the first third using hot set at an angle so as the edge becomes diagonal.

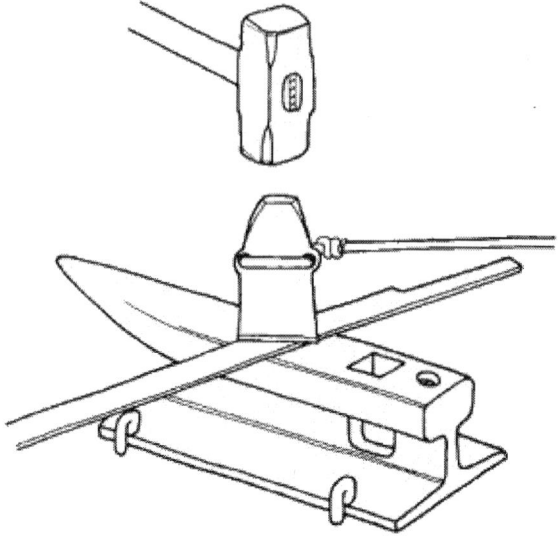

Diagonal edge;

Step 6: lay the cutting side on the anvil and draw the diagonally slanting sides, more so the angles to make them roundish

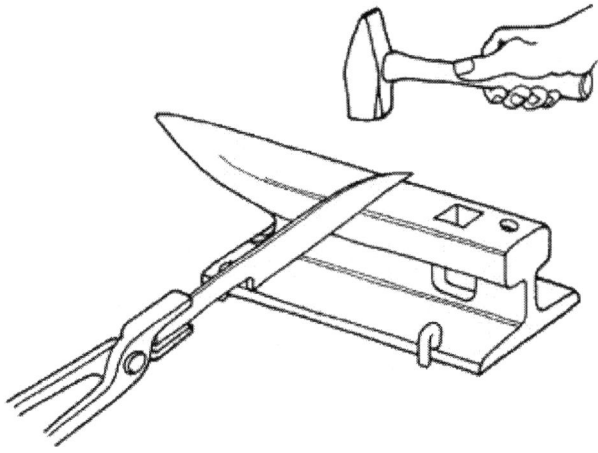

Step 7: now turnover upside down so that you can work on the other end to flow along the shape of the opposite end as shown below

Step 8: finish the knife blade by sharpening with a file

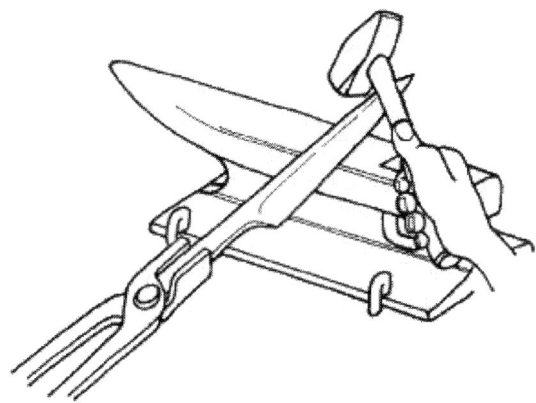

Step 9: harden and tamper as per the hardening and tampering technique

Step 10: you can opt to take to carpentry workshop to fix wooden handle.

Finished knife

Project 19: Axe head

Raw materials;

- High carbon steel.
- Used leaf spring can be used instead.

Tools required;

- Anvil
- Hammer
- Tongs
- Hot set
- Eye chisel

- Eye drift

Instructional steps

Step 1: forge a leaf steel and cut out slightly over half using hot set

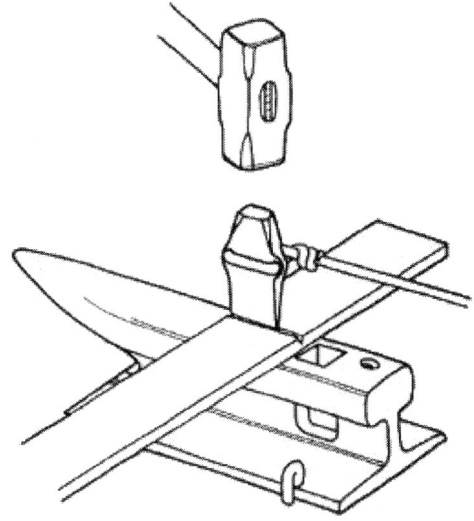

Step 2: cut the piece diagonally into two equal parts

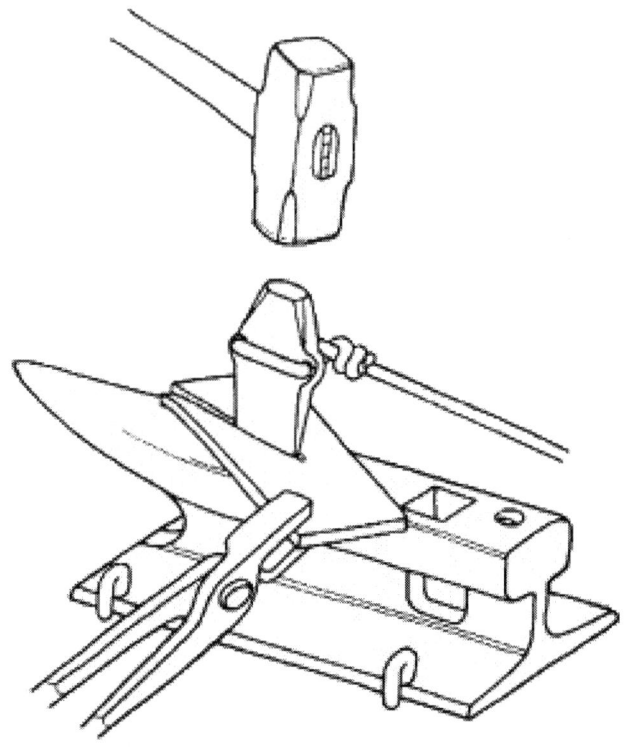

Step 3: forge one of the two pieces and trim off the sharp angles to pave way for roundish angles

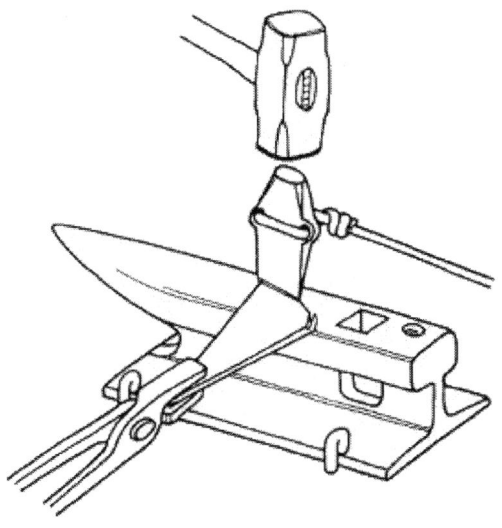

Step 4: hammer out the trimmed off pieces

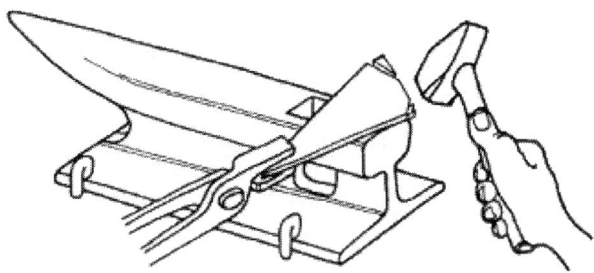

Step 4: rest the wider funnel like edge onto anvil and draw down towards the edge

Step 5: draw the narrow sides near blade edge to make even

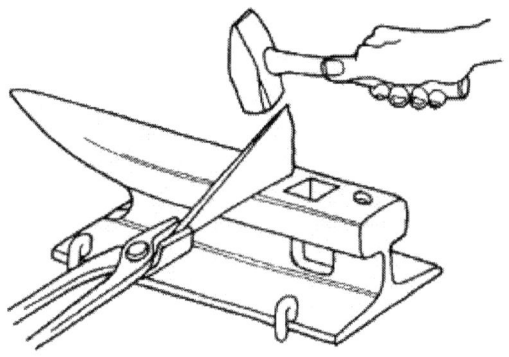

Step 6: round off the edges before reaching the ultimate thinness

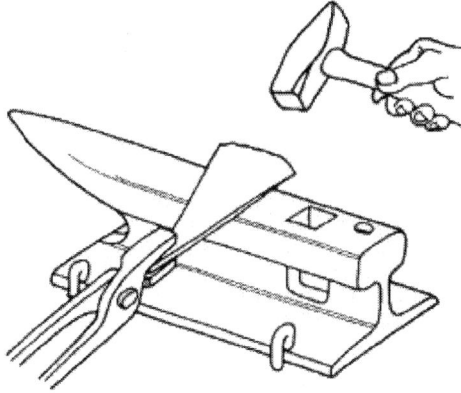

Step 7: continue drawing down at a slight angle to get an even angular edge

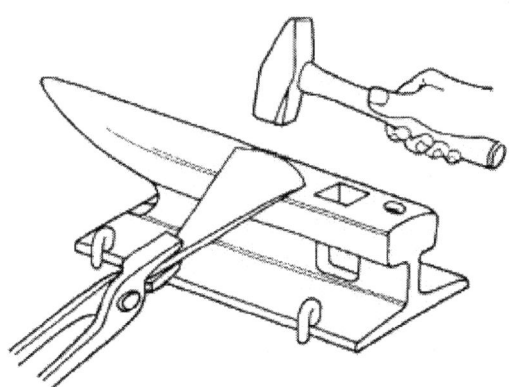

The finished axe blade

You can use folding techniques to bend the tang round to form some sort of a ring for the handle to enter. Use your carpentry workshop to prepare and insert handle.

Project 20: Hoe

Raw materials;

- Tractor plough disk

Tools required;

- Anvil
- Hammer
- Tongs
- Hot set
- Eye chisel
- Eye drift

Instructional steps

Step 1: Heat up the plough disk from center outwards

Step 2: mark two radii such as to take up a quarter of the disk and divide the marked part into two

Step 3: cut out a sector from the disc as shown below

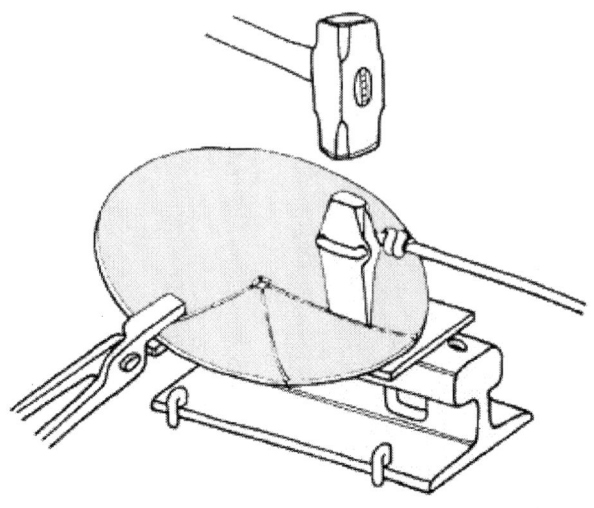

A disc sector to be used for making hoe blade

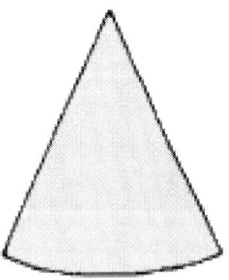

Step 4: draw out the tang to form a roundish handle

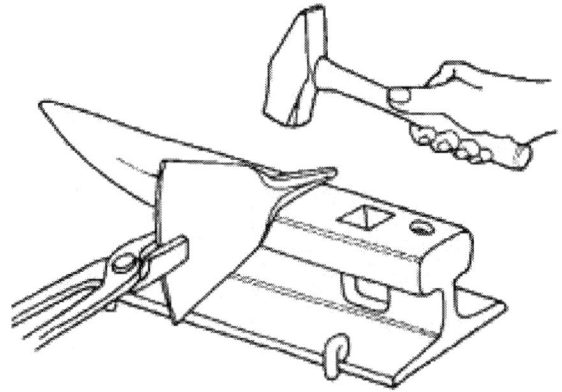

Hoe blade with an extended roundish tang

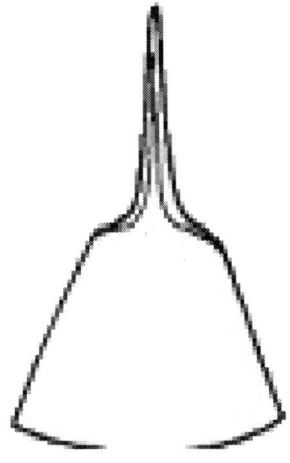

Step 5: finish off the hoe by drawing the blade section to get slant narrower and sharper at the edge

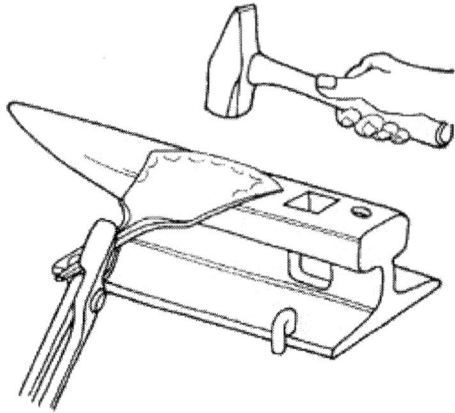

Hard and tamper as per the hardening and tampering techniques discussed earlier.

Like with axe blade, you can opt to forge and bend the tang to form a hole for the handle. Alternatively you can dig a hole just below the beginning of the tang for the handle and then cut off the tang's extension.

Conclusion

Thank you for downloading and reading this book.

This book has provided you with important details yet in the most basic approach to help you easily learn and use tools and resources abundantly available within your environment to become a creative and highly productive blacksmith.

In case you would like to advance to a great blacksmith, metallic workshop owner, metal fabricator, metallurgist, and even an industrialist in the fabrication, and structural construction industry, this is a great inspirational start.

It is my sincere hope that this book has helped you to become a skilled blacksmith and inspired you to utilize locally available tools and resources to better use in creating blacksmith products.

Again, thank you for downloading and reading this book. Please share with others information about it.

Thank you.

FREE Bonus Reminder

If you have not grabbed it yet, please go ahead and download your special bonus report *"DIY Projects. 13 Useful & Easy To Make DIY Projects To Save Money & Improve Your Home!"*

Simply Click the Button Below

OR **Go to This Page**

http://diyhomecraft.com/free

BONUS #2: More Free & Discounted Books or Products

Do you want to receive more Free/Discounted Books or Products?

We have a mailing list where we send out our new Books or Products when they go free or with a discount on Amazon. Click on the link below to sign up for Free & Discount Book & Product Promotions.

=> Sign Up for Free & Discount Book & Product Promotions <=

OR Go to this URL

http://zbit.ly/1WBb1Ek

Made in the USA
Columbia, SC
24 September 2018